what do we know and what should we do about...?

abortion?

titles in the series

What Do We Know and What Should We Do About Abolishing Prisons?
Joe Sim

What Do We Know and What Should We Do About Authoritarian Regimes?
Natasha Lindstaedt

What Do We Know and What Should We Do About Tax Justice?
Alex Cobham

What Do We Know and What Should We Do About Slavery?
Julia O'Connell Davidson

What Do We Know and What Should We Do About the Irish Border?
Kate Hayward

What Do We Know and What Should We Do About Social Mobility?
Lee Elliot Major and Stephen Machin

What Do We Know and What Should We Do About Internet Privacy?
Paul Bernal

What Do We Know and What Should We Do About Housing?
Rowland Atkinson and Keith Jacobs

What Do We Know and What Should We Do About Immigration?
Jonathan Portes

What Do We Know and What Should We Do About Inequality?
Mike Brewer

what do we know and what should we do about...?

abortion?

Tanya Saroj Bakhru
Grace E. Howard

S Sage

3rd Floor, HYLO
103–105 Bunhill Row
London, EC1Y 8LZ

2455 Teller Road
Thousand Oaks
California 91320

10th Floor, Emaar Capital Tower
2 MG Road, Sikanderpur, Sector 26
Gurugram, Haryana – 122002
India

8 Marina View Suite 43-053
Asia Square Tower 1
Singapore 018960

Library of Congress Control Number: 2025944809

British Library Cataloguing in Publication data

A catalogue record for this book is available from the British Library.

Editor: Rhoda Toweh
Assistant editor: Pippa Wills
Production editor: Martin Fox
Marketing manager: Maria Omena-Neale
Cover design: Victoria Bridal
Typeset by: TNQ Tech Pvt. Ltd.
Printed in the UK by Bell and Bain Ltd
BB0363636

ISBN 978-1-03-620137-1
ISBN 978-1-03-620136-4 (pbk)

contents

contents

about the series

Every news bulletin carries stories which relate in some way to the social sciences—most obviously politics, economics and sociology, but also, often, anthropology, business studies, security studies, criminology, geography and many others.

Yet despite the existence of large numbers of academics who research these subjects, relatively little of their work is known to the general public.

There are many reasons for that, but, arguably, it is that the kinds of formats that social scientists publish in, and the way in which they write, are simply not accessible to the general public.

The guiding theme of this series is to provide a format and a way of writing which addresses this problem. Each book in the series is concerned with a topic of widespread public interest, and each is written in a way which is readily understandable to the general reader with no particular background knowledge.

The authors are academics with an established reputation and a track record of research in the relevant subject. They provide an overview of the research knowledge about the subject, whether this be long-established or reporting the most recent findings, widely accepted or still controversial. Often in public debate there is a demand for greater clarity about the facts, and that is one of the things the books in this series provide.

However, in social sciences, facts are often disputed and subject to different interpretations. They do not always, or even often, 'speak for themselves'. The authors therefore strive to show the different interpretations or the key controversies about their topics, but without getting bogged down in arcane academic arguments.

Not only can there be disputes about facts but also there are almost invariably different views on what should follow from these facts. And, in any case, public debate requires more of academics than just to report facts; it is also necessary to make suggestions and recommendations about the implications of these facts.

Thus each volume also contains ideas about 'what we should do' within each topic area. These are based upon the authors' knowledge of the field but also, inevitably, upon their own views, values and preferences. Readers may not agree with them, but the intention is to provoke thought and well-informed debate.

Chris Grey, Series Editor

Professor of Organization Studies

Royal Holloway, University of London

about the authors

Tanya Saroj Bakhru is a Professor of Women, Gender, and Sexuality Studies at San José State University. She holds a B.M. in Violin Performance from the University of Redlands, an M.A. in Women's Studies from San Diego State University, and a Ph.D. in Women's Studies from University College Dublin. Dr. Bakhru's publications include *Reproductive Justice, Adoption and Foster Care with Krista Benson and the edited collection Reproductive Justice and Sexual Rights: Transnational Perspectives. Her research interests include Transnational Feminism, Reproductive Justice, and Feminist Critiques of Globalization.*

Grace E. Howard is an Associate Professor of Justice Studies at San José State University. She earned her Ph.D. in Political Science at Rutgers University, with concentrations in Women and Politics and Public Law. Dr. Howard has authored several published works, including *The Pregnancy Police: Conceiving Crime, Arresting Personhood*; "The Criminalization of Pregnancy Before and After Dobbs" in *The Routledge Companion to Gender and Crime*; and "The Pregnancy Police: Surveillance, Regulation, and Control" in *Harvard Law and Policy Review*. Dr. Howard's body of work explores reproductive law and policy, and the dimensions of legal personhood for people with the capacity for pregnancy. She is engaged in public scholarship on reproductive politics and law, with expertise on the criminalization of pregnancy, abortion, contraception, miscarriage, and eugenics. Her analysis and commentary have been featured in national and international news outlets including Huffington Post, BBC News, Telemundo, US News & World Report, Truthout, AP News, and NPR.

acknowledgements

Tanya: Thank you to Dr. Grace Howard for her collaboration and friendship on this project. I learned a lot from you throughout this experience. Deep appreciation goes to my family, in particular my spouse Tina McCauley and our son Finn. Tina, without your behind-the-scenes efforts and support, this project would not have been possible. I also want to acknowledge Dr. Daisaku Ikeda and the members of the SGI-USA, particularly the Bay Bridge Bay Island Chapter, for constant encouragement and support. Lastly, I write this book in dedication to all those who have struggled and continue to struggle for reproductive autonomy and bodily integrity for themselves and their communities. I will continue to do what I can to ensure that women and those with the capacity for pregnancy maintain control of their reproductive destinies.

Grace: First and foremost, I must thank my friend, colleague, and co-author Dr. Tanya Bakhru. Thank you for inviting me to co-author this book with you, for being the Order Muppet to my Chaos Muppet, and for keeping us on track despite the persistent horrors. I'm so excited that we get to have our names on a book together. Thanks also to Dr. Deirdre Condit and Dr. Cynthia Daniels for being the most encouraging (and also the most abortion-y) professors in undergrad and grad school. Both of you have changed my life in countless ways. I am also appreciative of Professor David Cohen for encouraging and supporting me since graduate school and for modeling academic advocacy. Thanks to Dr. Amanda Roberti for being my informed consent research comrade! I am forever thankful to Dr. Johanna Schoen and Professor Kimberly Mutcherson, both of whom have supported me in so many ways, first as a student and now as a professor, and whose series of intimate workshop-style conferences on abortion were groundbreaking, inspiring, eye opening. Thanks to Dr. Shelly Sella, who I first met at one of those conferences, and who treated me with such care and compassion when I shared about my time working in a bad abortion clinic for the first time. I will never forget the feeling of reassurance: that people needing abortions weren't alone in this. It was such an honor to share the stage with you so many years later. Deepest gratitude to Dr. Monica McLemore, who I also met at a Schoen-Mutcherson meeting. I am so privileged to call you family. Cheers to Meghan Eagen-Torkko, for teaching me about nurses and Catholicism and abortion, and for our mutual appreciation of cats and tight grapes. I must also thank Ash Williams, for sharing your revolutionary vision. Thank you to abortion funds, mutual aid groups, and practical support networks for holding it down and doing the things that need to be done. You are everything. We protect us! Thank you to my housemates at the Woman-sion, the feminist housing collective where I lived during my senior year of college, who bore witness to my own self-managed abortion. Thank you to everyone who has ever shared their abortion story, for your courage, and for showing us that abortion is normal. Thank you to abortion providers, who risk legal and physical harm to stand alongside people in their time of need. This book is dedicated to everyone who has had an abortion and to everyone who wanted to but couldn't.

1

introduction

Around the world 6 out of 10 unintended pregnancies and 3 out of 10 of all pregnancies end in abortion (World Health Organization, 2022). Contrary to popular belief, abortion is a common health care practice that in most cases is straightforward and safe. Access to comprehensive abortion care is so vital that it is one of the World Health Organization's essential health care services. It can be carried out by a range of health care workers through medication or a procedure. In fact, a medical abortion can even be managed by the pregnant person themself at home.

The danger of abortion lies not in the procedure itself, but in the social, political, and legal conditions under which it occurs. According to Haddad and Nour (2009), "Every year, worldwide, about 42 million women with unintended pregnancies choose abortion, and nearly half of these procedures, 20 million, are unsafe. Some 68,000 women die of unsafe abortion annually, making it one of the leading causes of maternal mortality (13%). Of the women who survive unsafe abortion, five million will suffer long-term health complications" (p. 122). As more people with the capacity for pregnancy face barriers to accessing safe, timely, geographically reachable, affordable, nondiscriminatory, and quality abortion services, they resort to clandestine and unsafe measures.

Time and again, research shows that restricting access to abortion does not reduce the number of abortions. However, restrictions on abortion do dramatically impact the safety and health outcomes for those seeking them. These include emotional distress and trauma, violation of human rights such as the right to privacy, the right to nondiscrimination, and the right to freedom from torture. Most tragically, unsafe abortion is a leading and preventable cause of maternal mortality.

Each of the authors of this book comes to the project with a passion and commitment to reproductive justice, human rights, and working for social justice across various intersections of identity.

Tanya: Reproductive justice and issues of bodily autonomy and sexual freedom are deep passions of mine. Our bodies are a core aspect of our identity and the place and space that generates how we move and experience the world. As a college student I came across Barbara Kruger's (1989) artwork "Your Body is a Battleground" (Caldwell, 2016). The idea of the body as a site upon which struggle, debate, contention, and even war take place resonated deeply. The body is both symbolic and material, figurative and literal. I knew this firsthand through my own experiences and those of my grandmother. The reproductive experiences of women and pregnant people's lives are both deeply personal and political.

My paternal grandmother was born in 1916 in the city of Rohri located in the Indian state of Sindh. Rohri is now in present-day Pakistan but had been a part of the British imperial project for hundreds of years. When my grandmother was married at the age of 14, her husband's family changed her first and last name. This was a common custom at the time and signaled a key shift: separate from her birth family, her obligation now belonged to her husband's family. A year later, my grandmother gave birth to a child who died in infancy. My father was born shortly thereafter.

At the time of the Partition of India in 1947, my grandparents and their four children lived in the city of Quetta. As my dad tells it, one night there was a riot in their town. Unrest between Muslim and Hindu groups had escalated as the end of British occupation drew near. My grandparents, my dad, his brothers, and sister hid anxiously in the

2

bathroom while fighting and rioting continued outside their home. The next morning, the British Army occupied the city, promising residents they would provide safe passage out of town so long as they left all their belongings behind. That night was the beginning of my family's yearlong journey as refugees—moving from Mumbai (Bombay) to Nagpur and eventually settling in Varanasi (Banaras). Once settled, my grandmother had two more children. Eventually in 1960 my father immigrated to the United States and sponsored, one by one, each of his family members to join him.

I think about my grandmother a lot. She passed away when I was 15. I don't know if my grandmother experienced anything firsthand but historians have noted that sexual violence and rape were a pervasive and prominent aspect of Partition and British occupation. It was likely that the number and spacing of her children were decided not by her but by her mother-in-law, as was the custom. I know based on stories handed down that my grandfather had a violent temper and was said to do things like throw his tea at my grandmother if she didn't bring it to him hot enough. I also know that in her later years she would have nightmares and wake up in the middle of the night screaming and that this stopped once my grandfather passed away. My grandmother always treated me with kindness and affection. She has a special name she called me and it seemed like whenever I saw her, she was cutting fruit and offering it to her children and grandchildren. What would reproductive freedom have looked like for her? How did she navigate a reproductive destiny that was shaped by so many personal and political factors? I have so many unanswered questions and try to excavate her story through interviews with my dad, aunts, and uncles. My grandmother's body was a battleground. Issues of domestic violence, colonization, patriarchal family structures, gendered expectations all played out on her body. It is for her and all women and pregnant people who strive for bodily autonomy that I commit my work.

Grace: My passion for reproductive justice grew out of my personal experiences with sexual violence and reproductive injustice. The man

I was dating sexually assaulted me when I was a sophomore in college. I remember sitting in my car in the grocery store parking lot the next morning, shocked, trying to figure out if I had enough money to buy emergency contraception (I did not). Having received virtually no quality sexual and reproductive health education in Virginia public schools, in the aftermath of the assault I found that learning about sex, sexuality, and reproduction was incredibly healing, validating, and empowering. It helped me feel ownership over the body that had been taken from me against my will. This knowledge helped me put into perspective the harms that had been done to me, and the cruel and nonsensical ways that we respond to sexual violence. Eventually, in doing this work, I felt honored when people in my community sought me out to accompany them through the aftermath of their own sexual assaults, when they asked me what to do about a suspected sexually transmitted infection (STI), or called me for advice on how to remove a slippery menstrual cup.

During this time, I was supporting myself with a handful of part-time jobs and had no health insurance. My family did not have the resources to help me. I was forced to rely on the free clinic at the department of public health office for healthcare, an experience that could be intimidating and even humiliating. Eventually, calling back to the tradition of second wave feminist consciousness-raising, I began to hold workshops on consent, sexual and reproductive health, cervical viewing, and how to advocate for oneself at gynecological (OBGYN) appointments.

At the beginning of my senior year of college, I noticed my period was late. I was pregnant, and did not want to be. An abortion would have cost around $350–$500, but I had only $5 to my name. So, with a lot of trepidation, I began to research alternative abortion methods, wondering which methods were most likely to work and least likely to hurt me. I had some kind of vague awareness that I could get in trouble for doing this, and gave my housemates instructions on what to say and do if I ended up needing emergency medical care. Whether it was a placebo effect, a coincidence, or the herbs had actually worked, I will never know. I do know that a few hours after I started the herbal regimen, I started bleeding. I was so relieved and felt so powerful and connected to my body. Reflecting on this moment, it was as close to a sacred experience as I have ever had.

After graduating from college, I trained as a birth doula and found a job working at a local abortion clinic. I donated my doula work to people who could not otherwise afford it. Through these experiences, I saw with my own eyes the many ways that pregnant people are belittled, trapped, violated, and objectified. I saw women who drove all night to make it to the 6 a.m. call time at the clinic, teenage girls who we had to send away because they were legally required to have a parent's permission for abortion in my state, and people who arrived at the clinic one day beyond the state's legal limit for abortion. I helped a woman give birth to a baby that she relinquished to another family after she was unable to get the abortion she wanted, and tried to intervene each time the nurses forgot to stop calling her "mama" instead of by her name. I saw, with my own eyes, how inadequate the pro-choice/pro-life framework was when applied to the full scope of our lives. And, I saw how, seemingly no matter the "choice" being made—birth or abortion—pregnant people couldn't seem to catch a break. I often joke that I got into this work because I followed my rage—rage about the ways I had been harmed, sexual assault, rage about the terrible things that were needlessly being done to people. I followed that rage and let it drive me through the times I felt beaten down, or hopeless, or tired. Behind that rage, there is a deep well of compassion, and the knowledge that all of this can be different.

These realities of preventable harm, unjust barriers, and needless suffering underscore that the greatest threats to abortion access are not medical, but structural. To truly understand and address these issues, we must listen to the lived experiences of those most affected and recognize that abortion is not only a health issue, but a matter of justice. For these reasons it is critical that the discourse surrounding abortion and consequent laws, policies, and procedures are informed by evidence based and factual information and research. Generally, social science research is concerned with the improvement of humanity, the elevation of basic dignity, and human rights. Social science research can enhance our understanding of the world by exploring and investigating new understandings of social issues. In this book we will examine the issue of abortion from a social science perspective, allowing us to make sense of the context of people's lived realities and envision a more just, equitable, and humane society.

This book contains three main chapters. The Background chapter examines the historical and cross-cultural constructions of pregnancy and abortion, revealing that these are not fixed biological facts but dynamic concepts shaped by power, culture, race, and technology. Drawing on ancient texts, traditional knowledge, and shifting medical authority, it traces how abortion has long existed, practiced through herbal remedies, midwifery, and, later, biomedical technologies. The chapter highlights the professionalization of medicine as central to criminalizing abortion and marginalizing midwives, often through racialized and gendered ideologies. It also explores how modern technologies like ultrasound and neonatal care have visually redefined fetal life, often in service of anti-abortion politics. Throughout, the chapter emphasizes that reproductive politics are not simply about choice or biology, but about contested narratives and institutional power over whose knowledge, experiences, and lives are valued.

The What Do We Know chapter offers a comprehensive global analysis of abortion as a critical issue at the intersection of public health, human rights, and structural inequality. It explores who has abortions, why, and under what circumstances, highlighting motivations such as economic insecurity, educational goals, health needs, and gender bias. The chapter also examines contemporary methods of abortion, the consequences of criminalization, and the disproportionate impact of abortion restrictions on marginalized communities, including LGBTQ+ individuals. It traces how abortion is entangled with histories of eugenics, colonialism, and population control, showing how state and institutional power have long shaped who is allowed reproductive autonomy. The chapter critiques disinformation campaigns and restrictive legal frameworks while emphasizing abortion as a safe and essential component of healthcare. Ultimately, it argues for a justice-based approach to abortion, one that centers dignity, equity, and bodily autonomy for all people, and recognizes abortion access as fundamental to gender equality and global health.

The What Should We Do chapter argues for a shift from individualistic, neoliberal notions of "choice" to a reproductive justice framework grounded in human rights, dignity, and intersectionality. It emphasizes that abortion cannot be understood in isolation from broader structural inequalities, such as racism, poverty, ableism, and patriarchy that shape reproductive lives. By centering the voices and experiences of marginalized people, the chapter underscores how reproductive justice links the right to abortion with the right to parent, bodily autonomy, and access to enabling conditions like housing, healthcare, and safety. Through case studies of the Jane Collective (U.S.), Repeal the 8th campaign (Ireland), and Joint Action for Reproductive Justice (South Korea), the chapter illustrates how grassroots, cross-movement organizing can achieve transformative legal and cultural change. These movements show that true reproductive freedom requires collective care, legal reform, and dismantling systemic barriers not just access to abortion, but the power and resources to make meaningful reproductive decisions.

background

Introduction

Constructions of pregnancy and consequently, of abortion, shift across time, culture, and political context. They reflect broader struggles over power, gender, race, medicine, and the body. This chapter explores how ideas about abortion have been shaped historically and cross-culturally not only by religious or moral beliefs but also by social change, colonialism, medical authority, and technological developments. We examine how abortion has been understood, practiced, and regulated, thus revealing that abortion has always existed, and its meanings and status have evolved in contested and often contradictory ways. In doing so, the chapter highlights a central theme of the book: that abortion in particular, and reproductive politics in general are shaped not just by individual choice or biological facts, but by deeply embedded cultural narratives and institutional power.

Historical continuities: Abortion across ancient cultures

People have always had abortions. Long before the advent of modern medicine, people found ways to intentionally end their pregnancies. Some of our earliest surviving examples of the written record, particularly medical texts, discuss and even instruct on how to achieve an abortion. As writer and activist Renee Bracey Sherman and journalist Regina Mahone write in *Liberating Abortion*, the Kahun Papyrus, the oldest surviving medical text in Egypt, dating back to 1800 BCE, includes a recipe for ending a pregnancy (2024, p. 78). The Ebers Papyrus, a compilation of ancient Egyptian medical texts, includes instructions for inducing abortion (Sherman & Mahone, 2024, p. 78). According to historian John M. Riddle, there is evidence that the Ebers scroll, written sometime between 1550 and 1500 BCE, is actually a copy of a much older version (1999, p. 35). "The prescriptions in this scroll date back to the Old Kingdom, a thousand years or more before the scribe copied what to take for upset stomachs, headaches, and yes, abortion" (Riddle, 1999, p. 35). Abortion was not only practiced in ancient Egypt. Sherman and Mahone assert, "some of the earliest medical records of abortion are believed to have been made by Emperor Shen Nung in Chinese mythology. He recorded an abortion recipe using mercury 4600 years ago" (2024, p. 77). The Indian *Sushruta Samhita* (600 BCE), a medical and surgical text discusses abortion to save the life of the pregnant person, and the *Pali Vinaya* (500–100 BCE), a legal text, discusses recipes and manual massage methods for abortion (Sherman & Mahone, 2024, p. 76, 84). Both Plato and Aristotle recommended abortion in some cases (Morrow, 2022).

Abortifacients and traditional knowledge

Ancient abortion methods typically involved the use of local plants, animal products, vigorous movement, insertion of objects into the cervix, and pressure from massage (Sherman & Mahone, 2024, p. 83). In Myanmar, Thailand, Malaysia, and the Philippines, belly massage was most prevalent; in Colombia, the herbs rue and basil (Sherman & Mahone, 2024). The San in southern Africa used a combination of herbs and physical exertion (Sherman & Mahone 2024, p. 90). The Taíno, the people native to the Caribbean, used the peacock flower (Sherman & Mahone, 2024, p. 90).

The Crow, an indigenous nation of the Great Plains in North America used calamus, tansy, and uterine massage (Sherman & Mahone, 2024, p. 94). As for effectiveness, Riddle asserts that "women thought that what they took worked successfully, and I found that modern scientific reports tend to confirm their practices as probably being effective" (1999, p. 7).

Entire books can and have been written on herbal abortion methods. For brevity, we will discuss two notable plants used for abortion, one with an extremely limited geographic range, and the other with a vast geographic range: silphium and juniper. Silphium, a member of the fennel family, grew in coastal Cyrene, a Greek colony in North Africa founded in 631 BCE (Sherman & Mahone, 2024, p. 84). Popular for both medicinal and culinary uses, silphium was such a commodity that its image was depicted on coins, showing the plant itself and also hinting at one of its medicinal applications with a woman gesturing at the plant and at her own belly (Sherman & Mahone, 2024, p. 84). Pedanius Dioscorides, a Greek pharmacologist from the first century AD, wrote that silphium could be used as a contraceptive and as an abortifacient, as did Soranus, a Greek practitioner and early gynecological writer in Rome in the first and second centuries AD (Riddle, 1999; Sherman & Mahone, 2024). Pliny the Elder, a Roman medical philosopher from the first century AD, wrote that the plant could be used to regulate menstruation, describing the plant as worth more than its weight in silver (Sherman & Mahone, 2024, p. 84). Fruitless attempts were made to cultivate silphium outside of Cyrene, and by the end of the first century, the plant was extinct—considered to be the first recorded extinction of a plant or animal species (Grescoe, 2022).

Juniper, on the other hand, has a wide distribution throughout the Northern Hemisphere and has been known to grow even at very high altitudes (Hampe & Petit, 2010). Juniper is also known as savin, the abortion tree, tree of life, lucky herb, bastard killer, plant of the damned, "kindermord" (German for child murder), and "jungfernpalme" (German for, a woman using the plant could pass as a virgin at her wedding) (Sherman & Mahone, 2024, p. 81). The Ebers Papyrus described Egyptian abortive uses of juniper mixed with pine resin (Sherman & Mahone, 2024, p. 81). Dame Trotula, a woman gynecologist from the 1100s in Salerno,

Italy, mentioned the use of juniper (Sherman & Mahone, 2024, p. 87). In the 1200s, Muslim physician and botanist Ibn al Baitar wrote that juniper would kill and expel a fetus (Sherman & Mahone, 2024). In the Great Plains in North America, the Crow used juniper as an abortifacient (Sherman & Mahone, 2024, p. 81; Theobald, 2019). Juniper was used in the British North American colonies as well (Reagan, 1997).

Contemporary biomedical abortion methods can be divided into two broad categories: procedural abortion and medication abortion. Procedural abortion is an intentional termination of pregnancy using medical instruments. Medication abortion involves taking pills orally or inserting them vaginally, enabling people to have their abortions at home. These methods will be discussed in greater detail in the next chapter of the book.

Social change, race, and the medicalization of abortion

Broader societal shifts have shaped constructions of pregnancy and abortion. For example, the late 1800s in the United States was a time of tremendous social and economic change, and this was also the era that saw the professionalization of medicine and the first abortion bans. As historian Sarah Dubow writes,

> Between the 1870s and 1920s, the places people lived and the jobs they worked, the clothes they wore and the foods they ate, the values they held and the facts they believed, the ways they spent their time and the ways they spent their money, the concerns they had and the hopes they held, all metamorphosed in ways that historians have characterized as the birth of modern industrial society (2010, p. 10).

Increased industrialization changed the structure of the family, drawing people, including young women, from rural areas to large cities, looking for employment in factories. The growing movement for Women's Suffrage, and white women's increasing participation in the wage labor force challenged existing notions that women belonged in the private, domestic sphere. Immigrants from Eastern and Southern Europe and China poured into the United States, while formerly enslaved people were now free to reproduce outside of the breeding programs of chattel slavery and without having their children sold away from them. Xenophobia and changing family norms fed the idea that white people were being outbred and would ultimately be replaced, a white supremacist concept still alive and well today, called Great Replacement Theory (Armstrong, 2003; Morone, 1997). Abortion was common during this period, either performed by midwives or self-managed by taking one of the many abortion medicines being manufactured and advertised at the time (Gutierrez-Romine, 2020).

Physicians hadn't been paying attention to the widespread use of abortifacients and contraceptives because at that time, they were largely uninvolved in pregnancy care (Sherman & Mahone, 2024, p. 109). Sexual and reproductive health was still largely left to midwives. In the mid-1800s, physicians embarked on a mission to professionalize and standardize medicine. By professionalizing medicine they could install themselves as the sole authorities on healthcare and eliminate their competition. They relied on nationalism and white supremacist beliefs of race suicide to make this possible. It is no surprise, then, that the first wave of abortion bans in the United States were accompanied by, and were a major strategy for, the professionalization of medicine.

While care from medical practitioners like physicians and nurses is ubiquitous in developed nations today, this was not always the case. Medical schools existed, but enrollment was generally limited to white men and was prohibitively expensive (even more so than it is today). It should also be noted that this was prior to the development and popularization of germ theory in the 1860s. As such, we should not assume that the care physicians had to offer in this early period was of higher quality than that of other "irregular" practitioners. As legal scholar Renée Ann Cramer writes, the legitimacy of physicians "rested on social status and access to higher learning and linked technical mastery with moral responsibility" (2021, p. 45).

Physicians (almost exclusively men) would not necessarily have received any training in sexual or reproductive health, which was largely considered the domain of women. Dr. James Marion Sims, known as the Father of American Gynecology, practiced (in the most literal sense of the word) at the first women's hospital in the United States, housed on a small slave farm in Alabama (Owens, 2017). Historian Deirdre Cooper Owens writes, "From 1844 to 1849, Anarcha, Betsy, Lucy, and nine other unidentified enslaved women and girls lived and worked together in the slave hospital" (2017, p.1). They were forced to endure repeated experimental gynecologic surgeries, with no anesthesia. If this is the power dynamic present at the founding of American Gynecology and Obstetrics, it is not surprising then that physicians in this field continued to work for the advancement of white supremacy and male domination.

The rise of patent medicine and abortion regulation

While there were certainly many skilled nonmedical healthcare practitioners at this time, there was also an explosion in "quackery." Historian Alicia Gutierrez-Romine writes, "Westward migration in the nineteenth century had created an opportunity for unlicensed medical practitioners to thrive beyond the major metropolitan areas associated with the professional class of physicians" (2020, p. 19). Before the 1906 Food and Drug Act, medicine in the United States was unregulated. A person could put any substance in a bottle, make claims about this substance being a miracle cure, and sell it perfectly legally. These were referred to as "patent medicines." Some of these medicines would have been legitimate and effective, but others could be completely ineffective or even dangerous. Historian Leslie Reagan writes, "the first statutes governing abortion in the United States [...] were poison control measures designed to protect pregnant women by controlling the sale of abortifacient drugs, which often killed the women who took them" (1997, p. 10). Some patent medicines were abortifacients: pills or tonics that would bring on a late period. The first anti-abortion measures in the United States were framed as consumer protection from this "pseudo-professional" class of irregular healthcare providers (Gutierrez-Romine, 2020, p. 21). For example, "the 1827 Illinois law, which prohibited the provision of abortifacients, was listed under 'poisoning'" (Gutierrez-Romine, 2020, p. 21).

It is within this context that physicians sought to differentiate themselves from these "irregular" practitioners. While in the United Kingdom, "medicine and midwifery are [. . .] inherently complementary [but] distinct professions," in the United States, midwives were "violently denounce[d]" (Cramer, 2021, p. 43). The American Medical Association (AMA) was established in 1847, seeking to educate the public about the dangers of irregular practitioners and to influence legislation that would regulate healthcare practice (Cramer, 2021). Only ten years after its founding, the AMA resolved to criminalize abortion at every stage of pregnancy (Dubow, 2010, p. 20). Dubow writes that, for physicians, "whose interest in the female reproductive system raised questions about their sexual morality, the anti-abortion campaign was a way to proclaim their own high morality in contrast to their competitors, their female patients, and even the ministers who tolerated abortion" (2010, p. 12). The AMA argued that abortion was both dangerous and immoral, especially when provided by nonphysicians (Fischer, 2016). However, their anti-abortion turn served another purpose as well: it would "eliminate an entire sector of practitioners from healthcare delivery"—the midwives (Fischer, 2016, p. 41).

Dr. Horatio Storer, "the preeminent face of the anti-abortion movement in the nineteenth century," was instrumental in criminalizing abortion in the United States (Gutierrez-Romine, 2020, p. 24). Making abortion a moral issue, and tying abortion to nativist fears about the survival of the nation and westward expansion, Storer asked, "'Shall' these regions [. . .] 'be filled by our own children or by those of aliens? This is a question our women must answer; upon their loins depends the future destiny of the nation'" (Reagan, 1997, p. 11). To promote his anti-abortion agenda, Storer attacked and discredited midwives and the idea of quickening as the beginning of life.

Quickening had long been considered the moment when life, or at least, meaningful life, began. Storer endeavored to change that, arguing:

quickening is as unlikely a period for the commencement of foetal life as those others set by Hippocrates and his successors [...] and false as them all [...] the mother and the child within her... must be entirely identical from the conception of later to its birth, or entirely distinct (Reagan 1997, p. 17).

Storer opted for "entirely distinct." By eliminating quickening, which Storer described as "but a sensation," physicians took the power to determine pregnancy away from the pregnant person, and into their own expertise (Reagan, 1997, p. 13). Reagan writes, "what had previously been understood as a blockage and a restoration of the menses prior to quickening was now associated with inducing a miscarriage by labeling it abortion. Furthermore, Storer equated abortion with infanticide" (1997, p. 13). Under Storer's leadership, the AMA's anti-abortion campaign successfully influenced legislation across the country, eliminating the common-law concept of quickening, and banning abortion throughout pregnancy (Reagan, 1997, p. 13). These laws included an exception: physicians could perform therapeutic abortions if they thought pregnancy and childbirth threatened the woman's life. "Physicians had won the criminalization of abortion and retained to themselves alone the right to induce abortions when they deemed it necessary" (Reagan, 1997, p. 13).

Technology and abortion

Technology has influenced the status of pregnancy and the fetus. Technologies that visualize pregnancy have transformed and made visible the hidden processes of embryological and fetal development. Medical advancements and the development of neonatology as a field have moved the "viability line" from around 28 weeks in 1973 to around 23–24 weeks today (Sella, 2025). While these technologies are ultimately neutral on questions of fetal personhood and bodily autonomy for pregnant people, they have also been deployed by anti-abortion advocates to serve their own political ends. In other words, the technologies themselves are neutral, but the meanings ascribed to these technologies are not.

Interest in the development of pregnancy, largely hidden from human eyes, is nothing new. Humans have long been interested in human gestation. Early visualizations of the fetus were hand-drawn in anatomical and midwifery texts from the 1400s (Callender et al., 2019). The first birth figures, drawings of developing embryos and fetuses inside the uterus, in a variety of different positions or presentations, were printed in 1513 (Callender et al., 2019). The fetus depicted in these birth figures resembles a fully developed, sassy-looking toddler (Whiteley, 2023). Even in these earliest iterations of visualizing the fetus, the birth figure did not necessarily provide "simple biological truths," but rather were embedded with "deep social and emotional significance for the early modern viewer" (Whiteley, 2023, p. 3). Indeed, as Historian Rebecca Whiteley notes, "birth figures [. . .] provided what women did not have: a picture of what was inside" (2023, p. 69).

By the 1930s, the general public would be invited to view a series of real human embryos and fetuses as a sideshow exhibit. At the 1933 Century of Progress World's Fair in Chicago, the "Masters of the Midway" Lew Dufour and Joe Rogers presented a sideshow called Life featuring "a graduated set of human embryos and fetuses" preserved in formaldehyde (Dubow, 2010, p. 28). The star attraction of this show was a jar containing a fetus with two heads (Dubow, 2010). At ten cents a ticket, the Life exhibit made more than $110,000 (Dubow, 2010). Dalfour explained, "there was money in the facts of life" (Dubow, 2010, p. 38). While these sideshow glimpses of the fetus suggest novelty and curiosity, fetal images have also been intentionally deployed to create an emotional response. Professor of Medicine Brian C. Callender, Historian Margaret Carlyle, and Professor of Obstetrics and Gynecology Julie Chor write, "By focusing on easily recognizable facial features, hands, or feet, often captured in evocative gestures, the anti-abortion movement has co-opted images to foster their contention [. . .] that the fetus is an independent entity deserving of legal and political protection" (2021, p. 1208). When making arguments about fetal personhood, anti-abortion advocates tend to shy away from some of the less baby-like qualities of embryos and fetuses, like the embryonic tail.

This imagery has even made its way into law and policy. Of the use of mandatory ultrasound in anti-abortion legislation, Callender et al. write that such laws "rely on notions that viewing the fetal ultrasound image will provoke or intensify maternal bonding and could reverse a person's decision to have an abortion" (2021, p. 1208). Many U.S. states require that patients seeking abortion care first view government-designed "informed consent" booklets which feature illustrations and photographs purporting to represent embryos and fetuses at two-week gestational increments. While informed consent is a standard part of abortion care, as it is a standard part of all ethical medical care, governments usually have no role in developing the content of informed consent materials or in requiring them by law. Political Scientists Cynthia Daniels, Janna Ferguson, Grace Howard, and Amanda Roberti's analysis of these booklets found that they are both inaccurate and misleading, consistently representing embryos and fetuses as more developed than they actually are (2016). In essence, the goal is that these materials will discourage people from having abortions once they have the "right" information. While the effectiveness of this strategy has been disproven (state-mandated informed consent for abortion does not change a prospective abortion patient's mind), it is a clear attempt to use visualization of the fetus not to merely inform but to influence (Joyce et al., 2009).

The work of Swedish photographer Lennart Nilsson has been hugely influential in our understanding of the fetus. Callender et al. write, "In April of 1965, fetal imagery entered the public sphere when Life Magazine published a photograph of a free-floating fetus on its cover with the title, 'drama of life before birth: unprecedented photographic feat in color'" (2021, p. 1208). These photographs isolated the embryo or fetus from its uterine surroundings, making it appear more separate and independent. Some of Nilsson's photographs depicted fetuses still inside the uterus. Others, though, were actually photographs of aborted embryos that Nilsson posed and manipulated to appear more baby-like. For example, in one photograph, he placed a fetal thumb into its mouth. These dead fetuses were being used to represent life.

While intrauterine photography is limited because of its invasive nature and the risks posed to the pregnancy, other methods of visualizing embryos and fetuses have been developed and have now become a routine part of medical prenatal care. The obstetric ultrasound transformed our ability to visualize the fetus, complete with printed or digitized copies of the image that the pregnant person could share with family, friends, or post to social media. Instead of quickening, Callender et al. write, "this initial personal and physical engagement with the fetus is now commonly replaced by the diagnostic experience of the ultrasound" (2021, p. 1209).

The first ultrasound images of a fetus were published in a 1958 paper in *The Lancet* (Donald et al.). By the 1970s, obstetric ultrasounds had become widespread. Sociologist Elizabeth Armstrong writes, "The relationship between the pregnant woman and the fetus was thus reconfigured, and the relationship between the pregnant woman and society was transformed as well" (2003, p. 194). In 1986, the first 3D ultrasound images of a fetus were taken, allowing full surface views instead of cross-sections (Campbell, 2013). By the 1990s, 4D ultrasound technology, which produces moving 3D images, made its debut (Campbell, 2013). As was the case with photographic visualization of the fetus, ultrasound images have been a powerful tool for anti-abortion advocates.

Viability

Generally speaking, fetal viability refers to the ability of the fetus to survive outside of the uterus. Definitions of viability will differ depending on whether we are discussing viability as a legal concept or as a medical concept. When viability determines whether or not a pregnant person has a right to end that pregnancy, the contours of the concept are worthy of examination. Legally, viability has been deployed as a rigid line associated with a specific gestational age that is applied to all pregnancies. Before the "viability line," abortion is permitted. After the viability line, it is not. Practically speaking, however, viability is not so rigid. Viability varies by pregnancy and by access to medical care. Some very advanced pregnancies are nonviable because the fetus has a lethal anomaly. Indeed, definitions of viability can even move beyond what is medically possible, instead relying on determinations made by the pregnant person. Dr. Shelly Sella, the first woman physician in the United States to openly perform abortions in the third trimester, writes, "Every patient who comes to me for an abortion has considered the factors relevant to their well-being and to their unborn child's and concluded that this particular pregnancy is nonviable" (2025, p. xviii).

Advancements in neonatal care have the power to shift the "viability line." In particular, infant incubators and artificial surfactant have vastly improved the likelihood that a preterm infant will survive. While these medical advancements should be celebrated for their ability to help babies, in a political context where fetal personhood is promoted and abortion is targeted for regulation or abolition, these medical advancements also pose some ethical considerations. Should every newborn be greeted with the full range of medical interventions, even if it is clear that these interventions will not be able to save the infant? If a newborn is going to die, should we allow that newborn to die in their mother's arms, or should we make every attempt, however futile, invasive, or painful, to keep that newborn alive? If a premature newborn could possibly survive at twenty-four weeks, should abortion be permitted at twenty-four weeks? (*See* Partridge, 2022).

Infant incubators are devices meant to protect the fragile bodies of newborns, especially low-birth weight or premature infants, infants who have fluid or meconium in the lungs, or infants who are recovering from trauma (Casper, 2022). In addition to regulating body temperature, incubators help to protect sensitive eyes and ears, regulate oxygen and humidity, protect from allergens, viruses, and bacteria, and can even come equipped with special lights to treat jaundice (Casper, 2022). First developed in France by Stéfane Tarnier in the late 1800s, infant incubators were meant to help tiny newborns that often died of hypothermia in cold hospitals (Casper, 2022).

Another advancement in neonatology was the discovery and synthesis of surfactant. As Sociologist Monica Casper writes, surfactant:

> reduces surface tension in the alveoli (air sacs in the lungs) where air and liquid meet. A deficiency of surfactant, such as when a baby is born prematurely, leads to higher surface tension and thus difficulty breathing. A premature infant can take one breath and exhale but cannot breathe in again as the lungs are likely to collapse (p. 114).

Pediatric researcher Mary Ellen Avery discovered the importance of pulmonary surfactant in the 1950s, while artificial surfactant was developed by Japanese pediatrician Tetsuo Fujiwara and was approved for use by the United States Food and Drug Administration in the 1990s (Casper, 2022). Synthetic surfactant has permitted the survival of infants born as early as 24 weeks gestation. It is on the World Health Organization's list of essential medicines (Casper, 2022).

Conclusion

In tracing the shifting constructions of pregnancy and abortion across cultures and time periods, it becomes clear that these concepts are neither fixed nor purely biological—they are deeply shaped by social, political, and technological forces. From ancient herbal knowledge and midwifery traditions to the professionalization of medicine and the deployment of fetal imagery, abortion has always existed, but its meaning and regulation have evolved. The rise of the medical profession, especially in the United States, was intimately tied to efforts to control reproduction, assert racial and gender hierarchies, and marginalize nonphysician practitioners like midwives. Technological innovations, such as ultrasound, have further transformed how pregnancy and fetal life are understood—often in ways that emphasize the fetus as separate from the pregnant person. While these tools are framed as objective or neutral, they are embedded with cultural meanings and have been mobilized to serve political ends. Ultimately, understanding abortion through a historical and cross-cultural lens reveals that what is at stake is not only a medical procedure but broader questions of autonomy, authority, and whose knowledge counts. As this chapter has shown, the power to define and control pregnancy has long been contested, and continues to shape abortion politics today.

what do we know about abortion?

Introduction

This chapter outlines the state of abortion in contemporary society from a global perspective. It addresses who has abortions, at what stages of pregnancy abortion occurs, why people have abortions—including the phenomena of sex selective abortion and son preference—and contemporary abortion methods in use. The chapter contextualizes the issue of abortion in the larger framework of state-imposed regulation of the body, and argues that criminalizing abortion does not, in fact, prevent or stop abortions from occurring.

The status of abortion worldwide

Understanding abortion at a global level requires attention to the intersections of race, gender, law, religion, economics, and politics. Abortion will always occur, whether it is prohibited by law or not. It is both a common occurrence and deeply contested practice. Abortion occurs across all countries, regardless of income or development status

(Hurst, 2020; Sommer & Forman-Rabinovici, 2019). In some regions of the world abortion access has expanded, while in others it has become more restrictive. Such disparities in the power and resources to access abortion parallels and exacerbates other global inequities: access to education, participation in the workforce, economic security, and freedom from coercion or violence. A global view of abortion reveals how the value assigned to different bodies and communities is shaped by their access to, or denial of, bodily autonomy. These disparities reflect broader patterns of power, control, and exclusion across political and cultural contexts.

In the last 30 years, we have seen overall decreases in desired family size, increases in the ideal age for starting a family, and shifts in cultural attitudes about the relationship between sex and reproduction. Notions of sex occurring outside marriage and for purposes other than reproduction have gained acceptance. As the Center for Reproductive Rights states:

> From Ireland to Nepal, abortion rights are becoming recognized as fundamental human rights for millions of people worldwide. And in Latin America, the Green Wave is ushering in a new era of liberalization in Colombia, Mexico, Argentina, and elsewhere in the region. (Center for Reproductive Rights, n.d.)

In the last 30 years, more than 60 countries and territories have liberalized their abortion laws. In fact, only El Salvador, Poland, Nicaragua, and the United States of America have increased restrictions on abortion in that time period. Approximately 60% of people live where abortion is broadly legal, leaving 40% of people to experience restrictive laws (Center for Reproductive Rights, n.d.).

In this global context, almost 73 million abortions occur every year. Although abortion is sought in both instances of intended and unintended pregnancies, it is estimated that six out of ten *unintended* pregnancies end in induced abortion, meaning intentional termination of pregnancy. While discussing abortion it is critical to keep in mind that official statistics on abortion might be incomplete due to issues of legality, differing reporting requirements between countries, or under-reporting. Regardless, abortion is a common intervention, and generally very safe when carried out in a medically approved method, and by a skilled practitioner.

Nonetheless, approximately 45% of abortions globally happen under unsafe conditions and cause preventable maternal deaths as well as physical and mental health complications, creating social and financial burdens for individuals and communities. This means roughly 25 million pregnant people have unsafe abortions each year. A team of researchers, Bearak et al. (2020), define unsafe abortion as a procedure for terminating pregnancy performed by persons lacking the necessary information or skills, and/or an abortion conducted in an environment that does not conform to minimal medical standards. In places where abortion is safe and legal, and contraception is widely available, the abortion rate is lower. These factors indicate that access to resources is necessary for bodily self-determination.

Abortion laws range from, on one end of the scale, absolute bans, to laws that restrict abortion to the context of saving the pregnant person's life or health, to bans that allow abortion in cases of fetal impairment reflecting social and economic values. On the other end of the scale, abortion laws can be written to allow abortion on demand, perhaps with gestational limits (Seager, 2018, p. 72). In some countries, including Bahrain, Indonesia, Kuwait, Malawi, Morocco, Qatar, Saudi Arabia, Solomon Islands, South Korea, Syria, Taiwan, Timor-Leste, Turkey, the UAE, and Yemen, a husband's consent is necessary to obtain an abortion. Rates of unintended pregnancies are highest in countries that restrict abortion access and lowest in countries where abortion is broadly legal. Therefore, regardless of its legal status, abortion is needed and sought (Guttmacher Institute, 2022a). In this context, abortion provision is increasingly acknowledged as an essential component of reproductive health services within global human rights frameworks, as recognized by the World Health Organization (2019).

Many factors circumscribe the use of and access to abortion. Legal, financial, and logistical constraints contribute to making some abortions unsafe or make safe abortions out of reach for many (Seager, 2018, p. 75). For example, during social or economic unrest, unintended pregnancies increase. Individuals and communities experiencing displacement are overwhelmed by the need for basic food, shelter, and safety, creating unique barriers to preventing unintended pregnancy for refugees. Disrupted family structures, exposure to sexual violence, and economic vulnerability complicate a pregnant person's relationship to their pregnancy and allowance of bodily autonomy. While unsafe abortion occurs globally, for those in resource poor regions of the world and in conflict zones, the need for sexual and reproductive health services is exacerbated.

In 1994, the UNFPA International Conference on Population and Development (ICPD) produced a groundbreaking Programme of Action that emphasized the importance of universal access to sexual and reproductive health and rights. This marked a significant shift away from population control narratives toward a more people-centered approach, highlighting bodily autonomy and the inextricable links between gender equality and positive reproductive health outcomes. Within this framework, abortion was recognized as a critical component of reproductive health. It exists within a broader system that includes antenatal, perinatal, and postpartum care; the provision of family planning services; the prevention and treatment of sexually transmitted infections (STIs); and the promotion of sexual health. These interconnected services are also deeply tied to broader dimensions of gender equity across economic, political, and cultural spheres (Guttmacher Institute, 2018; World Health Organization, 2024a).

While the Programme acknowledged the public health threat posed by unsafe abortion and emphasized postabortion care, it notably stopped short of calling for universal access to safe and legal abortion services (UNFPA, 1994). This omission, shaped by political and religious compromise, undermined feminist demands for full bodily autonomy and reproductive justice (Petchesky, 2003). By framing abortion primarily as a public health concern rather than a human right, the ICPD sidelined the lived experiences of those on the margins due to race, ethnicity, class, or age (Corrêa & Reichmann, 1994). The deference to national laws allowed conservative governments to maintain restrictive policies, perpetuating inequalities and unsafe practices (Cook et al., 2003). Feminist scholars contend that while politically strategic, this approach reinforced global hierarchies and failed to challenge the structural and systemic forces that limit reproductive freedom. Thus, despite its global significance, the ICPD's cautious language on abortion limited its transformative potential.

Barriers in legality, accessibility, and availability of abortion, delivered in a timely, affordable, respectful, and safe manner, compound mental and physical health risks for people with the capacity for pregnancy. Because pregnancy is time-sensitive, delays in abortion access, often due to legal restrictions, can increase the risk of medical and social harm. These restrictions can lead to lost educational and economic opportunities, worsen social and political marginalization, and result in medical complications including permanent reproductive damage, disability, or maternal death. It is estimated that roughly 39,000 deaths occur each year from unsafe abortions (Center for Reproductive Rights, n.d.).

Restrictions also contribute to distress, stigma, and violations of fundamental human rights, including the right to privacy, nondiscrimination, and equality. As the World Health Organization (2024b) states: "Regulations that force women to travel to attain legal [abortion] care, or require mandatory counseling or waiting periods, lead to loss of income and other financial costs, and can make abortion inaccessible to women with low resources" (Consequences of Inaccessible Quality Abortion Care). For these reasons, access to safe, timely, affordable, and respectful abortion care is a human rights and public health issue.

Globally, the majority of abortions are accounted for by women aged 20–24 years (Jones et al., 2023). In the United States, one in four people who can get pregnant will have an abortion in their lifetime (Jones et al., 2023). A common misconception is that most people who attain an abortion are teenagers who have never experienced pregnancy or birth. In reality, the majority of people who have abortions are already parents (60%), and are in their 20s (60%) (Jones et al., 2023). Almost two-thirds of abortions worldwide are accessed by married women. In the United States, people who obtain abortions are disproportionately low-income and marginalized. For example, about half of all people who have abortions in the United States live below the federal poverty threshold (Fuentes, 2023). While Black women make up 14% of women of reproductive age in the United States, they make up 28% of people who obtain the procedure (Fuentes, 2023).

The vast majority of abortions, 93.1%, occur in the first three months of pregnancy (Centers for Disease Control, 2022). Fewer than 1% occur in the third trimester. Abortion later in pregnancy almost always involves a wanted pregnancy and the discovery of a severe medical condition that affects the likelihood of survival, quality of life, or the pregnant person's health. Despite claims made by some anti-abortion advocates, abortion "up until the point of birth" is not a medical reality. Rather, the phrase functions as a political talking point designed to stigmatize abortion and justify restrictions later in pregnancy—despite the fact that such proced-ures are extremely rare and medically regulated. It distorts both clinical practice and legal frameworks to suggest a reality that does not exist (American College of Obstetricians and Gynecologists [ACOG], 2022).

Lack of access to safe and legal abortion care violates a range of human rights for women and pregnant people. "These include the right to life; the right to the highest attainable standard of physical and mental health; the right to benefit from scientific progress; the right to decide freely and responsibly the number, spacing, and timing of children; and the right to be free from torture and from cruel, inhuman, or degrading treat-ment or punishment" (United Nations, 1948; World Health Organization, n.d.-a). These violations are further compounded at intersections of gender identity, race, class, and geography, which create disproportionate bar-riers for ethnic and racial minority groups worldwide.

While abortion access is already a contested issue globally, LGBTQ+ individuals, particularly transgender, nonbinary, and queer people assigned female at birth, face additional barriers that are often overlooked or over-simplified in mainstream discussions of reproductive rights. These individuals may encounter stigma, systemic exclusion, and healthcare practices that fail to account for their specific needs. While individual experiences within the LGBTQ+ community are not monolithic, the community as a whole faces a wide range of barriers, including an increased burden of proof, repeated disclosure, and provider-level assumptions that can delay or block access to care. Nonetheless, the need for members of the LGBTQ+ community to have access to abortion exists for complex and varied reasons.

There is limited research highlighting abortion experiences and preferences of LGBTQ+ people (Lowik, 2022; Moeseson et al., 2021; Wingo et al., 2018). Laws and policies that restrict gender identity, sexual orientation, and expression—combined with restrictive abortion policies—can diminish the efficacy, safety, and accessibility of medically sound abortion care across gestational experiences. This includes related clinical interventions across gestational ages (World Health Organization, n.d.-b). Fear of discrimination, previous negative experiences, and culturally unresponsive care can discourage individuals from seeking services.

Queer women, transgender, and nonbinary people may encounter heteronormative assumptions when accessing care. In particular, those assigned female at birth who identify as transgender, nonbinary, and gender-expansive may face compounded barriers including stigma, homophobia, misgendering, financial obstacles, and a lack of culturally competent providers (Moseson et al., 2021). These barriers contribute to persistent health disparities and the presumption that LGBTQ+ people do not require abortion or reproductive healthcare.

In the United States, a recent study found that 12% of 18–34-year-olds identified themselves as falling into the category of transgender or gender nonconforming (Moseson et al., 2021, p. 376.e1). According to the Guttmacher Institute (2022b), as many as 16% of people who have abortions do not identify as heterosexual women. Among individuals assigned female at birth, a significant portion will require abortion care at some point in their lives. Transgender and gender nonconforming people *do* have abortions and, like others, may prefer medication abortion for reasons related to privacy, autonomy, and provider interaction (Moseson et al., 2021). According to Moseson et al. (2021), "many [people] prefer medication abortion over surgical abortion because medication is viewed as less invasive, offers greater privacy, and does not require anesthesia. Compared with cisgender women, trans, and gender expansive people may prioritize different factors in determining abortion method and preference" (p. 376.e2). They also found that this group of care seekers sought opportunities to manage abortions themselves at home without having to engage with protestors outside of clinics or clinic staff unfamiliar with LGBTQ+ issues, factored into their decision-making.

In a few instances, steps have been taken to improve LGBTQ+ inclusion in abortion care by signaling the importance of gender-affirming, trauma-informed care models. For example, in 2023, the Canadian government renewed funding for Health Canada's Sexual and Reproductive Health Fund (Government of Canada, 2023)—initially launched in Budget 2021—and committed $36 million over three years to support research and projects aimed at expanding abortion services and addressing access barriers for marginalized populations, including rural and remote residents, Indigenous communities, and members of 2SLGBTQI+ groups (Government of Canada, 2023). Two-Spirit (2S in 2SLGBTQI+) is a term used by some Indigenous North American communities to describe a person who embodies both masculine and feminine spirits, or fulfills a distinct cultural gender role. It is a culturally specific identity rooted in Indigenous traditions and histories. Drawing from World Health Organization guidance, Health Canada's Sexual and Reproductive Health Fund frames sexual health as "an integral part of overall health, well-being and quality of life... not merely the absence of disease, dysfunction, or infirmity" (Government of Canada, 2023; adapted from World Health Organization, n.d.). This framing positions sexual and reproductive health not as reactive or optional, but as central to public health and human rights policy.

This commitment has materialized through several targeted initiatives supported by the Sexual and Reproductive Health Fund. Projects like *Improving the Quality and Access of SRH Care for 2SLGBTQI+ People*—developed in partnership with Sherbourne Health in Toronto—received funding to develop, pilot, and promote peer-reviewed and evidence-based training for healthcare providers working with 2SLGBTQI+ communities on family planning, pregnancy, parenthood, and general sexual health with culturally responsive models of care (Government of Canada, 2023; Sherbourne Health, 2023). Another initiative *Access for All* led by Action

Canada for Sexual Health and Rights, expanded the *Access Line*, a program offering financial and logistical support for people forced to travel for abortion services and improving sexual health information for those facing complex barriers to care (Government of Canada, 2023).

Moving toward a LGBTQ+ inclusive abortion services and advocacy globally requires more than funding alone. It means centering the lived experiences of people from this community and restructuring how abortion is framed and discussed. Advocates, policymakers, and healthcare providers must use inclusive language when speaking about abortion rights and sexual and reproductive health in general. The rights and restrictions surrounding abortion impact all pregnant people, not only those who identify as women. Experts also note that meaningful LGBTQ+ inclusion requires addressing abortion within an intersectional framework that simultaneously confronts racial inequality, economic marginalization, disability, political exclusion, and broader concepts of bodily autonomy and freedom (Whelan, n.d.).

As stated previously, abortion laws vary significantly across the globe. While some countries (e.g., Canada, Nepal, and South Africa) allow abortion on broad grounds, others (e.g., El Salvador, Malta, and the Philippines) have complete bans (Center for Reproductive Rights, 2024). Despite legal restrictions, abortion rates are similar in countries where it is legal and where it is not—what differs is the safety of the procedure (WHO, 2021). Even in legally permissive environments, access is often hampered by costs, travel distance, provider shortages, and fear of legal reprisals—especially for young people, refugees, and rural residents (Singh et al., 2018). While globally there is a trend toward liberalizing abortion laws, a persistent worldwide movement of anti-abortion activism and ideology poses a serious threat to abortion experience and, within the human rights framework, to the bodily integrity of pregnant people, their families, and communities. Across regions, these anti-abortion movements share ideological roots in religious conservatism, nationalism, and "traditional" gender norms, using political, legal, and cultural strategies to restrict both reproductive and other bodily rights. Ideological drivers like patriarchy, control of female sexuality, and religious morality have facilitated an alignment between right-wing populist and nationalist movements.

In a study by Amnesty International (2021), researchers identified four key strategies used by anti-abortion actors to undermine reproductive freedom. One of the most insidious is the use of *toxic narratives and conspiracy theories* to frame gender equality and LGBTQ+ rights, or abortion itself, as a threat to 'traditional values.' These narratives not only rely on fear-based terms like 'genderism,' 'gender ideology,' or 'prenatal genocide,' but also strategically invert the discourse by portraying feminists, queer theorists, and progressive advocates as the true sources of misrepresentation and disinformation. In this rhetorical inversion, those advocating for bodily autonomy are cast as ideologues manipulating public opinion, while anti-abortion forces position themselves as protectors of moral clarity. The result is that dominant actors, often those in positions of political, religious, or social influence, consolidate their authority by reframing themselves as the threatened party. In doing so, they co-opt the language of vulnerability and redirect public sympathy, reinforcing existing power structures under the guise of moral defense.

For example, in Poland, religious and political conservatives promoted panic over the fabricated threat that "genderism"—a term imposed on, not derived from progressive theory—framing it as a threat to the Polish family and national values. The far right successfully linked progressive conceptions of gender to chaos, moral decay, and even pedophilia, despite simultaneous revelations of child sex abuse within the Catholic Church in Poland (Graff, 2014). This inversion not only neutralized the language of rights but redirected public scrutiny away from institutional power and onto those advocating for inclusion.

The second strategy proposed by Amnesty International, *disinformation campaigns*, refers to the prevalence of social media and digital platforms to spread misleading or manipulative content. These campaigns compound both the speed and scale of disinformation, often blurring the lines between fact and opinion. According to Amnesty, these tactics weaponize medical "concern" to ask misleading questions or sow fear, for example, by suggesting that abortion increases cancer risk or mental illness, or falsely linking abortion to child abuse (Amnesty International, 2021, p. 14). A prominent example is Heartbeat International, a U.S.-based organization that funds so-called crisis pregnancy centers globally to dissuade people from accessing abortion care or reliable information on the subject, to surveil prospective abortion-patients, and even to mislead people about the status of their own pregnancies. Amnesty International (2021, p. 14) highlights surveillance of prospective abortion patients, while Open-Democracy (2020) discusses worldwide misinformation networks that mislead people about the status of their own pregnancies.

The third tactic named by Amnesty International is *the restricting of civil society space,* which makes gathering and implementing culturally meaningful change more difficult, if not impossible. For example, decreasing NGO funding and increasing bureaucratic hurdles and administrative requirements creates legal and financial burdens that obstruct the functioning of civil society organizations. These tactics are used to limit the operational capacity of advocacy networks under the guise of neutrality. Buyse, from the Netherlands Institute of Human Rights, outlines many examples of such examples, including restrictions on creation, registration, and legal recognition of civil organizations in Tanzania, Afghanistan, Egypt, and Russia (2018).

Finally, the fourth strategy, *targeted attacks on women's human rights providers and advocates* describes stigmatization, which includes efforts to discredit, stigmatize, and question the ethics or legitimacy of organizations or individuals. These tactics undermine the authority of new voices by sowing doubt, confusion, and internal division. The Amnesty International Report, *Challenging Power, Fighting Discrimination* offers a clear example: In 2014 and 2015, in response to El Salvador's blanket abortion ban, members of Agrupación Ciudadana por la Despenalización del Aborto (civic group for the decriminalization of abortion) and La Colectiva Feminista para el Desarrollo Local (feminist collective for local development) were accused of being "unscrupulous," "pro-death," "unpatriotic traitors," and of "manipulating vulnerable women" for leading campaigns to defend women imprisoned for obstetrics emergencies and accused of murder. It was even insinuated that their defense of these women and girls could encourage others to commit infanticide (Amnesty International, 2021). This strategy is also exemplified by violence against abortion providers. In the United States, the National Abortion Federation has recorded the incidents of anti-abortion violence against affiliated abortion providers and clinic staff from 1977–2024, including: stalking (781), death threats (1,652), assault and battery (570), bioterrorism threats (668), invasion (505), arson (203), bombing (42), attempted murder (26), and murder (11) (National Abortion Federation, 2025). It should be noted that these numbers represent an undercount, as they only include reported incidents from NAF affiliated clinics.

Abortion is a global public health and human rights issue deeply shaped by intersecting forces of gender, race, class, geography, and politics. While progress has been made toward liberalization and inclusive care, significant disparities remain in access, safety, and legal protection. There remains an urgent need for comprehensive, rights-based reproductive healthcare. To ensure bodily autonomy for all, abortion must be understood not in isolation, but as part of a broader struggle for gender equality, health equity, and freedom from violence, stigma, and discrimination across the globe. Centering these realities is not just a matter of health policy or legal reform, it is a commitment to structural justice, and to ensuring that no one is left navigating their reproductive future in silence.

Motivations for abortion

People seek abortion care for a wide range of reasons, yet dominant political and cultural narratives often oversimplify—or misrepresent—those decisions. Furthermore, forming a complete picture of global motivations remains difficult due to inconsistent laws, varying degrees of enforcement, and limited mechanisms for cross-cultural reporting of intimate, sensitive data. In a major study in the United States, the most frequently cited reason for abortion is that continuing a pregnancy would interfere with education, work, or a person's ability to take care of other dependents, reported by 74% of respondents (Finer et al., 2005). Other reasons included not being able to afford a baby (73%), not wanting to be a single parent or having relationship issues (48%), or feeling they had completed childbearing (33%). Respondents were able to select multiple reasons, illustrating how abortion decisions reflect overlapping and often compounding motivations (Finer et al., 2005).

Despite the variety of motivations and the imperfect data, public discourse frequently centers abortion care as a matter of moral choice or social failure, or sometimes coercion or selective pressure, while ignoring the complex broader economic, social, and familial realities that shape people's decisions. Globally, individuals seek abortion care for multidimensional reasons, including financial constraints, family planning, or educational and employment goals. In some contexts, faith may also shape abortion decisions—sometimes as a source of internal reflection, communal ethics, or spiritual discernment. While often excluded from policy discourse, faith-based reasoning can coexist with critical thinking and multidimensional care logic. Research in sociology and anthropology shows that religious belief and active critical judgment often coexist in decision-making. For instance, scholar Amy Adamczyk (2008) found that religion's influence on women's attitudes toward abortion was significant, but not determinative of their actual choices.

Across social and geographic contexts, economic insecurity is a leading reason people seek abortion across income levels. The cost of raising a child, lost opportunities for financial advancement, lack of government support, and poverty often influence reproductive decisions (Singh et al., 2018). In a study by researchers at the Guttmacher Institute, Chae et al. (2017), authors examined official statistics across 14 countries and found that economic reasons were consistently cited regardless of social stratification, political structure, or fertility rate. Respondents also shared that younger people—particularly adolescents and students—may seek abortion because they lack the financial means to raise a child or fear that a child would interfere with future opportunity (Chae et al., 2017).

Economic factors influence reproductive decisions not only in times of acute crisis but also during periods of relative stability. Because poverty often follows a cyclical pattern, individuals are forced to make repeated economic calculations throughout their reproductive lives. Economic insecurity can intensify suddenly, through natural disasters, war, or displacement, and often overlaps with chronic vulnerabilities such as domestic violence, housing instability, or political upheaval (United Nations Population Fund [UNFPA], 2023). Even when conditions appear stable, the recurring nature of poverty ensures that reproductive choices remain under economic pressure. Therefore, the need for abortion access during and after instability is not an exception, but a predictable structural necessity. Recursion here refers to the way poverty and crisis regenerate themselves across time, constraining autonomy long after the immediate emergency has passed.

Ensuring access to abortion in such contexts is not merely a matter of individual choice; it is foundational to a resilient human rights framework. As the United Nations Population Fund notes, "Women and children account for more than 75 percent of the refugees and displaced persons at risk from war, famine, persecution and natural disaster; 25 percent of this population at risk are women of reproductive age and one in five is likely to be pregnant" (UNFPA, 2023).These patterns are echoed at the individual level in reasons cited for abortion across diverse contexts. Chae et al. (2017) found that most women sought abortions in response to con-strained material, social, and familial conditions—not out of abstract preference, but due to tangible pressures like economic insecurity, partner absence, fear of stigma, or the need to care for existing children. While such reasons may appear discrete, they frequently co-occur and reinforce one another, reflecting broader systemic forces. The data suggest that abortion is rarely an isolated decision—it often represents a structural negotiation within recursive conditions of instability, inequality, and con-strained agency.

Additionally, people with the capacity for pregnancy frequently cite interruption of education or career opportunities as a reason for abortion (Chae et al., 2017). This is particularly relevant for adolescents, students, and people in precarious employment. Many people seek abortion due to unstable relationships or because they have completed their desired family size. Globally, 61% of unintended pregnancies end in abortion, often as a considered aspect of fertility planning (Bearak et al., 2020). The younger a person is when they have their first child, the younger they are when they reach desired family size, causing a situation where a focus on controlling fertility and limiting pregnancy goes on for the remainder of a person's reproductive life. In places where other forms of contraception are unavailable, abortion becomes a method to prevent unwanted or unintended pregnancy (Bankole et al., 1998).

Contrary to common political rhetoric, less than 1% of individuals cite coercion by family or partners as the primary reason for abortion (Guttmacher Institute, 2016). Studies affirm that most abortion decisions are internally motivated and deeply reflective. In many cultural contexts, abortion is highly stigmatized. This stigma limits open dialogue, delays care, and can result in unsafe procedures (Berer, 2004). The coercion myth further silences people's voices and delegitimizes their autonomy. Abortion decisions are complex, personal, and often shaped by systemic challenges rather than coercion. Misrepresenting these choices undermines the dignity and autonomy of those who seek care.

For these reasons, abortion must be understood as a healthcare and human rights issue, not a moral or political battleground. Abortion-seekers' experiences must be centered in policy debates (Ross & Solinger, 2017). Governments must ensure abortion is legally available, affordable, and accessible. This includes removing waiting periods, mandatory counseling, and criminal penalties (Center for Reproductive Rights, 2024). Public health systems should offer comprehensive reproductive care, including contraception, maternal care, and postabortion services (WHO, 2021). A global, justice-oriented approach to abortion recognizes reproductive rights as fundamental human rights and promotes structural change that supports—not restricts—people's capacity to make empowered choices.

The motivation to seek abortion can also be shaped in part by cultural attitudes toward women and girls. In some countries particularly in South, East, and Central Asia, economic and cultural structures produce a preference for sons and a corresponding devaluation of daughters. The less value women have, the fewer resources are invested in girls, reinforcing the diminishing status of girlhood and reconfirming the preference for boys. In patrilineal families, sons typically reside with their parents while daughters marry into their husband's household, which means families see little long-term gain in having daughters and may feel pressure to divest girls as soon as possible.

Even as countries implement legal reforms to address sex-based inequities, sons often retain exclusive economic planning and inheritance rights, allowing gendered asymmetries to persist. These preferences are reinforced through family name inheritance, religious customs, and planning for financial security in old age. Global trends in declining family sizes and restrictive government policies often unintentionally exacerbate the pressure to have sons, especially in contexts where cultural and economic structures already devalue daughters. For example, China's One Child Policy, Vietnam's Two Child Policy, and India's Two Child Norm have put more pressure on parents to give birth to males (Rahm, 2020, p 15). These policies are examples of state-driven population control measures shaped by demographic, political, and socioeconomic concerns. China's One Child Policy (1979–2015) strictly limited most families to one child to curb population growth, enforced via incentives and penalties (Hesketh et al., 2005). Vietnam's Two Child Policy, introduced in the 1980s, similarly promoted small families through propaganda and administrative sanctions (Guilmoto, 2012). India's Two Child Norm is a nonmandatory guideline encouraged through policies like eligibility restrictions for elected officials in some states (Visaria, 2000). As a result, abortion of female fetuses remains prevalent in these regions, along with female infanticide and the neglect of girls (Nanda, 2018; for a discussion of infanticide in the West see also Lewis, 2025). The high rates of sex-selective abortion in India and China have contributed to seriously skewed gender ratios in both countries (Nanda, 2018; Rahm, 2020).

Beyond individual family preference, research by political sociologist Rahm (2020) shows that son preference is shaped by gendered economic roles and legal norms around family balancing, reinforcing cultural expectations that sustain gender bias over time. In South Korea, India, and Vietnam, three primary motivations for sex-selective abortion are consistently identified: (1) prevention of sex-linked genetic disorders, (2) family balancing, especially when prior children are of the same sex, and

(3) cultural or economic preferences for sons. While some of these factors may appear neutral or health-related, they often reflect deeply rooted social inequalities that favor male offspring.

From a human rights perspective, gender-biased sex selection is considered a harmful practice because it reflects entrenched preference that deliberately prevent the birth of female children. "The practice is explicitly linked to discriminatory social norms and is identified as a malignant outcome of gender inequality" (UNFPA, 2020 p. 42). It is a part of an entrenched gender inequality impacting societies worldwide. The UNFPA states

> Gender-biased sex selection is the termination of a pregnancy when the fetus is determined to be female, or pre-implantation sex determination and selection, or 'sperm-sorting' for in-vitro fertilization. China, India, Nepal, South Korea, Singapore, Viet Nam, Armenia, Azerbaijan, Georgia, Albania, Montenegro, Kosovo, and Tunisia are all countries with historically skewed sex ratios at birth. Despite policy efforts, persistent cultural and economic incentives for sons—especially in India and China—continue to drive disparities in birth outcomes (UNFPA, 2020).

Historically, families seeking sons often relied on postnatal methods—female infanticide, abandonment, or deliberate neglect of female infants—to ensure male lineage continuity. These practices are now broadly condemned, at least outwardly, but the underlying pressures have not disappeared. Instead, they have shifted underground or re-emerged in new forms. With the development and wider availability of prenatal sex-determination technologies, reproductive choices have moved earlier in the pregnancy timeline. Social policy now operates in the space between moral objection and reproductive autonomy, often determining whether a choice is considered regulated family planning or prohibited discrimination.

With the rise of prenatal screening, medical technology has shifted the timeline of sex selection from postnatal to prenatal (Rahm, 2020, p. 18).

While these technologies have significantly improved reproductive outcomes and autonomy, they have also enabled earlier sex selection. In
particular, ultrasound technology gained widespread use in the 1970s and
became routine by the 1980s. As it became more affordable and portable,
access expanded beyond upper social classes to include those in urban
and rural settings, as well as those with fewer financial resources. This
expansion allowed a broader range of families to make reproductive
decisions based on fetal sex-shaping demographic trends in ways that
echo longstanding preferences for sons.

Starting in the early 1990s and continuing through the present-day
efforts began to address the negative impacts of sex selection and
resulting sex ratios at birth. Government intervention came in various
forms including: an increase in laws addressing gender equality around
issues of inheritance or property such as the 2005 Hindu Succession Act in
India; campaigns to change cultural attitudes about the value of girls and
address gender discrimination such as the Care of Girls campaign in
China; the promotion of adoption; reducing policies that regulate family
size, such as a relaxation of the One Child Policy in China; and in the form
of legal bans on the use of ultrasound or abortion for the purposes of sex
selection such as the Medical Service Act in Korea or Population Ordi-
nance in Vietnam (Rahm, 2020, p. 63 ; Ganatra, 2008).

However, no single action or policy has been successful in reducing son
preference. There is no evidence that banning ultrasounds or abortions is
directly linked to a reduction in sex-selective abortion or in son preference
more broadly. In fact, singling about bans on ultrasounds and abortion for
the purposes of sex selection creates additional health barriers for women
seeking care, makes health care providers less likely to provide critical and
needed abortion care, can cause patients to seek unregulated and unsafe
abortion care outside regulated channels, and reduces women's status
overall which further incentivizes son preference. It also gives individual
service providers and governments reasons to monitor and control all
abortions regardless of the reason and fosters an overall anti-abortion
climate such as in India after the passing of the Medical Termination of
Pregnancy Act (Ganatra, 2008).

In 2012, five UN agencies, the Office of the High Commissioner for Human Rights, the United Nations Population Fund (UNFPA), the United Nations Children's Fund (UNICEF), UN Women, and the World Health Organization (WHO) issued a statement saying that:

> States have an obligation to ensure that these injustices are addressed without exposing women to the risk of death or serious injury by denying them access to needed services such as safe abortion to the full extent of the law. Such an outcome would represent a further violation of their rights to life and health. (OHCHR, UNFPA, UNICEF, UN Women, and WHO, p. 5)

Addressing sex ratio imbalances is a complex issue. Sex-selective abortion reflects deep-rooted gender inequality reinforced by cultural, social, and economic structures. Despite legal reforms and public campaigns, the preference for sons persists. To address the root causes of son preference a comprehensive approach rooted in gender equity, cultural change, and human rights is essential to redress these imbalances and value all children equally.

Methods of abortion

Quality abortion care is defined by the WHO as "care that is: effective, efficient, accessible, acceptable/patient centred, equitable and safe" (World Health Organization, 2022, p. 21). Quality abortion care requires accessibility in terms of timeliness, cost, geographic location and with skilled attendants along with consideration for service users' culture, community practices, and individual preferences. Worldwide, there are multiple methods for performing abortion which vary depending on factors including legal status of abortion, healthcare infrastructure, and cultural stigma. The two main methods of abortion—procedural (sometimes referred to as surgical) and medication—vary in safety and accessibility depending on legal status, health care infrastructure, cultural stigma on abortion access and method preference, yet both are essential components of reproductive healthcare.

Procedural abortion can take on different forms. The procedures typically involve a healthcare provider numbing and dilating the cervix, and then using instruments or a suction device to empty the contents of the uterus (National Abortion Federation, 2024). Most procedural abortions involve variations in opening or dilating the opening of the cervix (the os) so that the contents of the uterus can be removed. There are different methods of procedural abortion that are appropriate for different stages of pregnancy, different fetal and maternal indications and, especially in cases where the abortion is performed on a wanted but nonviable pregnancy, the preference of the pregnant person.

The most common abortion procedure is vacuum aspiration abortion. This can be performed using an electric vacuum aspirator (EVA), or a manual vacuum aspirator (MVA). Typically provided through 14–16 weeks from the last menstrual period (LMP), aspiration abortion uses gentle suction to empty the uterus (National Abortion Federation, 2024). First, the patient may receive an anti-inflammatory medication, pain medication, or even general anesthesia. Next, local anesthesia is injected into the cervix, and a series of increasingly larger dilation rods are used to gradually open the cervix. Then, a flexible tube, or catheter, is inserted into the cervical opening, and gentle suction removes the embryo or fetus and placenta. Finally, the provider will examine the tissue to ensure that everything has been removed, and the patient can begin to recover. An electrical vacuum aspiration abortion can be performed in less than five minutes.

Another procedural abortion method, dilation and curettage (D&C) is like vacuum aspiration, but instead of inserting a catheter and applying suction, a curette, sort of like a long spoon, is inserted into the uterus through the dilated os (National Abortion Federation, 2024). The curette is used to gently scrape the sides of the uterus to dislodge and remove the pregnancy. Before the use of vacuum aspiration, D&C was the primary procedural abortion method in early pregnancy. Now, it is more likely to be used after 14 weeks LMP, after other abortion methods have failed, or as treatment for an incomplete abortion or miscarriage. Though still incredibly safe, D&C carries a higher risk of infection or uterine perforation than vacuum aspiration, as it requires greater cervical dilation, and the repeated insertion of a rigid metal instrument into the uterus.

Dilation and evacuation (D&E) is a procedure typically performed after 14 weeks of pregnancy (National Abortion Federation, 2024). This procedure is also typically performed as an outpatient service and takes no more than 30 minutes. After around 14–16 weeks LMP, the most common abortion procedure is D&E. At this stage of pregnancy, the cervix needs to be opened a little bit wider to accommodate the more developed pregnancy. This can be performed with dilation rods or with osmotic dilators— substances, inserted into the os, that swell as they absorb fluid. Laminaria, a type of seaweed from the kelp family, was first used as an osmotic dilator by Japanese physicians in the late 1800s (Wantanabe et al., 2011). It is still used by some physicians today, though synthetic alternatives have been developed as well. If using osmotic dilators, these are inserted the day before the abortion (National Abortion Federation, 2024). After the cervix is dilated, the patient is sedated or given an epidural, and then medical instruments like the curette, forceps, and vacuum aspiration are used to remove the contents of the uterus. A medication is then given to help the dilated uterus to contract. The procedure takes about 10–20 minutes.

Dilation and Extraction (also known as intact D&E or D&X) is another abortion method typically reserved for pregnancy after 20 weeks LMP (Chasen et al., 2004). At this stage of pregnancy, the fetal head has undergone a period of significant growth. This would require a much greater degree of cervical dilation—so much so that the cervix could be injured. As such, the D&X involves dilating the cervix, removing the fetus feet-first, piercing the fetal skull so that it could be compressed enough to fit through the dilated cervix. This abortion method is also used in cases where the fetus has developed hydrocephalus, a condition where the fetal skull grows up to two-and-a-half times its typical size due to a buildup of fluid in the brain cavity.

In the United States, this abortion method is heavily politicized. Anti-abortion organization National Right to Life coined the term "partial birth abortion" to stigmatize this abortion method (Esacove, 2004). According to the American College of Obstetricians and Gynecologists, dilation and extraction is "safest and offers significant benefits for women suffering from certain conditions" (ACOG, 2015). This abortion method was banned, except "when the woman's life is endangered." Alternatives to D&X are more time consuming, risky, invasive, and potentially trauma- tizing, including inducing early labor and giving birth vaginally, removal of the uterus, incision into the uterus, and nonintact D&E, where the fetus is instead removed in pieces, increasing the risk of infection, uterine perfo- ration, and incomplete abortion.

Medication abortion uses pills instead of procedures to induce abortion (National Abortion Federation, 2024). Medication abortion may be completed using one or two substances and used until 24 weeks of pregnancy. The first method involves taking a medication called mife- pristone, which cuts off the hormones that support a pregnancy, and 24–48 hours later, taking four tablets of a medication called misoprostol, which causes uterine contractions. The second method involves using additional doses of misoprostol, taken over several hours, to dislodge and expel a pregnancy.

Some people prefer medication abortion because it avoids a medical procedure, can feel more natural than a procedural abortion, and the abortion itself occurs in the privacy of a person's own home. One disad- vantage is that medication abortions can take between several hours to several days to complete. In recent years in the United States, medication abortion has become the most common abortion method, accounting for 53% of abortions in 2020 (Jones and Friedrich-Karnik, 2024). This number has increased to at least 63% in 2023, a year after the overturning of Roe v. Wade, the Supreme Court case that found abortion to be a fundamental constitutional right (Jones & Friedrich-Karnik, 2024).

Misoprostol was originally developed in 1973 to treat gastric ulcers (Löwy & Corrêa, 2020). A synthetic prostaglandin, misoprostol causes cervical softening, dilation, and uterine contractions. By the 1980s, misoprostol became known as an abortifacient. The common story of how this came to be is that feminists in Brazil, seeing the "don't take this when you are pregnant" labels on the medication, learned that this affordable, over-the-counter pill could terminate a pregnancy (Braine, 2023). However, according to writer and activist Renee Bracey Sherman and journalist Regina Mahone, this innovation actually came from drugstore vendors "who recognized its additional uses and the women they recommended it to, who risked their lives to test its consistency and spread the word throughout Brazil" (2024, p. 97). As it turns out, the Brazilian drugstore vendors were on to something. By 2012, the World Health Organization published a protocol for a misoprostol-only abortion (Raymond et al., 2023). The current WHO guideline for misoprostol-only abortion before 13 weeks LMP calls for 800 μg misoprostol (four pills) taken every three hours, for a total of twelve pills over the course of six hours (Obstetric and Gynecological Consultative Committee, 2018).

Mifepristone was developed for the French pharmaceutical company Roussel Uclaf by French scientist Étienne-Émile Balieu in 1980 (Baker, 2024; Calkin, 2023). Mifepristone is what Balieu called an "anti-progesterone," blocking the hormone progesterone that is needed to sustain a pregnancy (Baker, 2024, p. 12). When used in conjunction with a prostaglandin, this could terminate a pregnancy. First known as RU 486 (RU for Roussel Uclaf), it was approved for use in France in 1988, despite pressure from anti-abortion advocates (Baker, 2024). According to Carrie Baker, Professor of American Studies, by 1999, mifepristone was approved for use in Austria, Denmark, Finland, Germany, Greece, Luxembourg, the Netherlands, Spain, and Switzerland, and within a decade was approved for use in 28 other countries, including the United States (2024, p. 14).

In the United States, the Food and Drug Administration or FDA has approved the use of mifepristone and misoprostol to terminate a pregnancy up to 10 weeks LMP (FDA, 2025). However, the World Health Organization asserts that it is safe through 12 weeks LMP, and some studies have indicated that it is safe and effective through 15 weeks LMP (Kapp et al., 2021). To induce an abortion, you first take 600 mg of mifepristone, then, 24 to 48 hours later, you take 400 mg misoprostol either inserting the pills vaginally, sublingually (under the tongue), or buccally, (by putting four misoprostol pills between the gum and the cheek, two on each side of the mouth) and allowing them to dissolve (American College of Obstetricians and Gynecologists, 2020). Inserting the misoprostol vaginally can mitigate the nausea sometimes caused by the medication. However, especially if the legality of the abortion is in question, the vaginal route is not advised, as the pills may leave detectable residue in the vagina (Baker, 2024). If taken by mouth, mifepristone and misoprostol are currently undetectable by blood or urine test (Baker, 2024).

When performed under proper medical conditions, abortion is an extremely safe procedure. Serious complications from abortions that follow medical guidelines are rare. Although legal status and abortion safety are not always one and the same, there is substantial evidence showing that countries with restrictive abortion laws have higher rates of abortion-related morbidity and mortality than in those countries with more liberal abortion laws (Sedgh et al., 2012). Furthermore, in countries with prohibitive abortion laws, the collection of data can be incomplete. Safe and comprehensive abortion care should be seen as one step in a con-tinuum of care that includes preabortion services such as physical health checks, informed consent, and counselling, and postabortion/follow-up care. As the World Health Organization states, "Comprehensive abortion care includes the provision of information, abortion management including induced abortion, and care related to pregnancy loss/spontaneous abor-tion and post-abortion care" (WHO, 2022, p. 21). For people with the capacity for pregnancy, having the opportunity to discuss questions and concerns and receive support in their decision making is critical. According to The National Academies of Sciences, Engineering, and Medicine (2018), individualized, sensitive, and respectful communication; cultural sensi-tivity; support for emotional and other needs as they arise; and confir-mation that the abortion decision is voluntary (not coerced) are all essential aspects of safe and comprehensive abortion services. Ensuring access to safe, comprehensive, and culturally sensitive abortion care is vital to reproductive health. Both procedural and medication abortions, when provided under appropriate conditions, are highly safe and effective.

Respecting individual needs and autonomy must remain central to abortion care in policy, practice, and global health frameworks.

The regulation of abortion

The regulation of abortion is one aspect of the regulation of bodies and sexual behaviors. Institutions, such as medicine, religion, school, family, media, and governments, both local and national, participate in the regulation of bodies and behaviors (Puri et al., 2011). Through various social and legal mechanisms like laws, policies, and choices about financial expenditure, institutions exert power to signal which bodies and behaviors are normal or abnormal, legitimate, or illegitimate, and which bodies should be allowed self-determination and which should not (Briggs, 2017; Ross et al., 2016; Solinger 2001, 2013). The regulation of bodies in this way is one aspect of social control. In this context the regulation of abortion is not unique. This section of the book will trace the connection between the regulation of sexual behaviors, birth, abortion, eugenics, and population control.

Eugenics is a Greek word that translates to "well born." In the late nineteenth century and into the early twentieth century, a pseudoscience was built around the idea that social traits were heritable, and that mankind could achieve utopia with thoughtful and intentional breeding. Sir Francis Galton named this pseudoscience "eugenics." Influenced by philosophies of racial hierarchy and social Darwinism, eugenicists believed that those deemed the most fit by society should reproduce as much as possible (positive eugenics) while those deemed socially unfit should not reproduce at all, and should be prevented from doing so (negative eugenics).

In the United States at the end of the nineteenth and beginning of the twentieth century, fears of a falling white birth rate, social shifts driven by industrialization, immigration, and the emancipation of enslaved people, eugenicists believed that intentional breeding was the only way to prevent the downfall of white America. They believed that poverty, lasciviousness, queerness, and criminality, for example, were all traits that could be passed from parent to child. People with physical and developmental disabilities, epilepsy, and substance abuse disorder were also seen as socially undesirable. These people, eugenicists believed, should be prevented from reproducing, against their will if necessary. Influenced by Gregor Mendel's work on dominant and recessive traits with pea plants, eugenicists believed that people who appeared socially adequate could be secretly carrying "unfit" genes that had the power to ruin an entire family line. Family pedigree charts became an essential part of eugenic pseudoscience.

The first eugenic sterilization law in the world was passed in Indiana, the United States, in 1907 (Gould, 1985). By the 1920s, eugenics was all the rage in the United States, and it began to show up in law and policy. One Virginia hospital superintendent, Dr. Albert Priddy, an ardent eugenicist, sought to sterilize members of families deemed to be unfit (Lombardo, 2008). After a failed attempt to involuntarily sterilize and institutionalize members of the Mallory family—an impoverished white family accused of having operated a brothel out of their home—and a lawsuit brought by the patriarch of the Mallory family, Dr. Priddy was shaken. He wanted a law that would support his endeavors to prevent future trouble. Dr. Priddy got his law. Written by Harry Laughlin, superintendent of the Eugenics Record Office, this model legislation was adopted in Virginia in 1924 (Gould, 1985). According to this law, people could be sterilized against their will if it was thought to be for their own good. Carrie Buck would be the first candidate for eugenic sterilization under the new law.

Carrie Buck was placed in foster care with the Dobbs family after her mother, Emma, was institutionalized—the Bucks were desperately poor, and Emma, mother to three children by two different men, was unmarried—this, alone, was considered proof of Emma's unfitness. A member of the Dobbs family raped Carrie, and she became pregnant as a result. To spare the family from the shame and embarrassment of being guardian to an unmarried pregnant girl, Carrie was placed in the same institution as her mother as soon as her pregnancy began to show (Gould, 1985).

Carrie gave birth to her daughter Vivian while institutionalized (Gould, 1985). Vivian was taken from her and placed with the Dobbs family. Carrie never saw her again. When Vivian was still a baby, she was examined by a social worker who determined that the child was strange in some ambiguous way—something the worker admitted could have been influenced by her knowledge of Vivian's family history (Gould, 1985). This was enough evidence for Dr. Priddy to decide that the Buck family line was tainted: three generations of unfit women. Carrie was selected to be the first candidate for eugenic sterilization under the new eugenics law. She was also more or less selected to be the test case for eugenic sterilization laws at the US Supreme Court.

Eugenics was popular throughout western Europe, each national eugenics movement with its own specific agenda focused on curbing inherited degeneracy and race mixing. Influenced by American eugenics law, Alberta (Canada), Sweden, Norway, Denmark, and Germany adopted their own eugenics laws (Klautke, 2016; Stern, 2022; Strange & Stephen, 2012; Tydén, 2012). Though the Third Reich's eugenics policies and the Holocaust would eventually become the best known examples of eugenics at work, German eugenics had grown out of the U.S. eugenics movement. One superintendent of a eugenic institution lamented "the Germans are beating us at our own game" (Klautke, 2016). One of the first laws put into place after Adolph Hitler became dictator of Germany was a eugenic sterilization law: the law for the prevention of hereditary diseased offspring (gesetz zur verhütung erbkranken nachwuchses) in 1933 (Klautke, 2016). This law established over 200 eugenic courts, and required all doctors to report patients who were intellectually or physically disabled, mentally ill, blind, deaf, epileptic, or alcoholic (Pfafflin, 1986). Between 300,000 and 450,000 people were forcibly sterilized by the start of WWII in 1939 (The Biological State). The Nazi regime deployed other eugenic strategies as well: placing undesirables in concentration camps and carrying out the mass murder of Jews, Roma, political dissidents, queer people, and people with disabilities. The Aktion T4 euthanasia program resulted in the murder of around 70,000 people who had been held in institutions or who had birth defects (Hepburn, 2014).

Eugenic sterilization was also incredibly popular in Japan under Emperor Hirohito (Otsubo & Bartholomew, 1998). The Japanese government was concerned about the quality of the Japanese gene pool. Laws for the prevention of leprosy were used to segregate undesirables in sanitariums, which practiced sterilization and forced abortion. The Konoe government's National Eugenic Law of 1940 resulted in the sterilization of around 25,000 people by 1995 (Hurst, 2019). The 1948 Eugenic Protection Law allowed for the sterilization of people convicted of crimes, people with genetic diseases including color blindness, hemophilia, alcoholism, ichthyosis, people with epilepsy, and people with mental. illnesses like schizophrenia and manic depression (Hurst, 2019). This law was ruled unconstitutional in 2024.

The debunking of eugenics has unfortunately not ended state attempts to influence and shape their populations with forced sterilization and other population control measures. People with HIV, especially women, are a common target for forced sterilization, purportedly to prevent the transmission of HIV to the fetus (Bi & Klusty, 2015). However, there are now medications that can prevent the transmission of HIV to a pregnancy, which undermines the stated purpose of this strategy. HIV positive people face forced sterilization around the world, including in Chile, the Dominican Republic, Mexico, Namibia, South Africa, and Venezuela. One common coercive tactic is the withholding of medical services until a patient agrees to be sterilized. This includes withholding AIDS medication and assistance with birth.

Disabled people globally continue to be a target population for forced sterilization, even after eugenic thought began to fall out of favor after WWII. Justifications for sterilizing disabled people include: thinking they have no control over themselves, not wanting to deal with menstruation, and the terrible reality that rape of institutionalized disabled women is not uncommon (Human Rights Watch, 2011; National Women's Law Center; Open Society Foundation, 2011). Queer people are another targeted population for forced sterilization, based on an understanding that LGBTQ people are mentally ill and that intersex people are deformed (Open Society Foundation, 2015). Many countries require sexual sterilization of intersex people and of trans people seeking to have their legal documents updated or to receive gender–affirming medical treatment. In 2024, the Czech Constitutional Court found forced sterilization laws to violate European Union human rights law (Lopatka, 2024).

Racial and ethnic minorities, especially indigenous people, have been targeted for sterilization worldwide, arguably as a genocidal colonization tactic. The Roma people have been targeted in the Czech Republic, Hungary, and Slovakia. The Quechua and Aymara people in Peru and the Inuit in Greenland have all been targets of state sterilization programs (Open Society Foundation, 2011). In Israel, Ethiopian Jews were unwittingly given contraceptive injections to prevent them from reproducing (Abusneineh, 2021). In the United States, Black women (especially in the South) were primary targets for sexual sterilization through the 1960s, as exemplified by the case of the Relf sisters—two sisters in Mississippi whose family sued after they were sterilized against their will (Roberts, 2014). Between 1970 and 1976, an estimated 25–45% of women of reproductive age who came for healthcare at Indian Health Service facilities in the United States were sterilized (Lawrence, 2000; Theobald, 2019). Latina immigrants were sterilized against their will in Los Angeles between 1971 and 1974 (Stern, 2005). In 2020, nurse Dawn Wootin disclosed her concern about forced sterilization of immigrant women being held in detention centers in Georgia (Higgins, 2020).

These efforts to control reproduction—through sterilization, coercion, or criminalization—reflect broader struggles over bodily autonomy and the politics of personhood. Just as states have historically regulated who may reproduce, they have also shaped beliefs about when life begins and what constitutes a pregnancy, abortion, or moral transgression. While today, many anti-abortion advocates view abortion as the taking of an "unborn life," this perspective has not always been the case. Beliefs about when a fertilized egg, embryo, or fetus counts as, or becomes, a person have shifted significantly over time, even within a single political or religious group or single society. It is generally hypothesized that humans recognized the connection between sex and pregnancy after the emergence of agriculture, in part through working with domesticated animals. Determining whether someone was pregnant, however, was a trickier matter.

Before the invention of more reliable pregnancy testing in the 1900s, it was difficult to know if a missed period was a pregnancy or something else. The cessation of menses could indicate any number of things. Historian Rickie Solinger writes, "Doctors and midwives agreed that menstrual irregularity—in fact, all the symptoms of pregnancy—*could* be associated with conditions other than pregnancy" (Solinger, 2019, p. 12). A missed period was seen as a blockage or an obstruction that "required attention" (Reagan, 1997, p. 8). Historian Alicia Gutierrez-Romine writes that a woman would not have been "faulted for attempting to remedy the obstruction" (Gutierrez-Romine, 2020, p. 18). Bringing on a late period was not considered an abortion, but rather, returning the body to a state of balance (Reagan, 1997, p. 8). Historian Leslie Reagan writes, "if an early pregnancy ended, it had 'slipp[ed] away,' or the menses had been 'restored'" (Reagan, 1997, p. 8).

Pregnancy could not be confirmed until "quickening," or the pregnant person's experience of the sensation of fetal movement. While every pregnancy is different, quickening typically happens around four months or 16 weeks from the last menstrual period. It was thought that quickening indicated the moment of "ensoulment," or the fetus gaining a human soul (du Prey, 2008; Scott, 1996). Quickening is an ancient concept, addressed by philosophers such as Aristotle (though his timing was off—Aristotle believed that male fetuses quickened at 40 days and females quickened at 80 days) (Dubow, 2010). Prior to quickening, ending a pregnancy or restoring the menstrual flow would not have been considered a crime. It is notable that under the quickening standard, only the pregnant person has the power to determine whether they are pregnant. As Reagan writes, "the popular ethics regarding abortion and common law were grounded in the female experience of their own bodies" (Reagan, 1997, p. 8).

The Catholic Church endorsed the quickening standard. Christian philosopher Saint Augustine believed that a soul could not inhabit an unformed body, and so quickening rather than conception marked the moment of ensoulment (Dubow, 2010, p. 19). Other Christian theologians also endorsed this standard. Third-century theologian Tertullian wrote in his *Treatise on the Soul* that "in this matter, there is no more fitting teacher, judge, witness, than one of this sex. Reply, you mothers, you bearers of children, let the sterile and the masculine be silent. The truth of your nature is sought" (Dubow, 2010, p. 19). This continued through the twelfth-century. Dubow writes that quickening "was confirmed as Catholic dogma in 1312, when the Council of Vienne adopted St. Thomas Aquinas's endorsement of Aristotle's theory of ensoulment or 'delayed hominization'" (Dubow, 2010, p. 19). The Catholic position on abortion only changed from the quickening standard to the conception standard in 1869, when Pope Pius IX removed the distinction between pregnancies that had quickened and pregnancies that had not. Abortion performed at any stage of pregnancy became an excommunicable offense (Dubow, 2010, p. 19).

Other religious traditions have their own moral standards on abortion. For example, in Islam, the fetus becomes a person 120 days after conception (around four months, incidentally, around the time that quickening begins) (Dubow, 2010, p. 6). In Judaism, life begins at birth (Dubow, 2010, p. 6). In Hinduism and Buddhism, life does not exactly begin or end: "conception and death are not the boundaries of life" (Dubow, 2010, p. 6).

Contemporary conflict around abortion frequently rests upon fetal protectionism and the maternal-fetal conflict: the idea that the pregnant person and the fetus are separate entities with conflicting interests. The maternal-fetal conflict assumes that the pregnant person is the primary threat to their own pregnancy. By inventing an adversarial relationship between the pregnant person and the fetus, the government is given a reason to restrict the pregnant person's autonomy in favor of protecting the "innocent" fetus. Fetal protectionism generally rests on the assumption that third party intervention in a pregnancy is necessary to represent the best interests of the fetus, because the pregnant woman is unwilling or unable to do so.

Applying the theory of the maternal-fetal conflict has resulted in the involuntary detention of pregnant people in medical facilities, prisons, and jails; forced medical interventions and denial of medical interventions; nullification of advance directives; and even keeping brain dead bodies on life support to gestate pregnancies (Howard, 2024; Paltrow & Flavin, 2013; Sherman, 2025). The maternal-fetal conflict is the logic that assigns attorneys and legal guardians to represent the interest of the fetus in cases of judicial bypass for abortion, where juveniles who are legally required but unable to get permission from their parents to have abortions, must appeal to a judge for that permission (Silverstein, 2001). The pregnant juvenile is not granted legal representation, but the fetus may be. The maternal-fetal conflict leads to blaming and punishing people for their pregnancy losses.

It is important to note that banning or criminalizing abortion does not make it go away. Studies have consistently shown that globally, people have abortions regardless of legality. One recent study found that the abortion rate (per 1,000 women) was 41 under broad legality, and 39 where prohibited altogether (Bearak et al., 2020). Abortion bans do, however, place people who are seeking abortion in legally, and some-times physically, precarious positions—reliant on clandestine providers or unregulated medications. Patients seeking postabortion care may be turned away from hospitals or arrested and prosecuted. Examples abound of the harm done by criminalizing abortion and of people's will-ingness to go to great lengths to procure one anyway. Many groups were involved in helping people access abortion care during this period of criminalization. And while the criminalization of abortion meant that many of these groups operated more or less underground, the Clergy Consultation Service on Abortion (CCS) is an example of one that operated more openly (Danielsen, 2021; Frank, 2025; Frank et al., 2023; Schoen, 2019).

Founded in 1967 by nineteen ministers and two rabbis, the CCS was "the first organization in the United States to publicly offer abortion referrals" (Dirks & Relf, 2017, p. 3; Sherman & Mahone, 2024, p. 56). On May 22, 1967, the New York Times published an article on the front page announcing that the CCS would help women access safe abortion care (Dirks & Relf, 2017). One CCS-Cleveland member, Reverend Farley Wheelwright, explained to the Wall Street Journal, "This is no abortion underground[...] We're helping to bring abortion above ground, to make it open, respectable, and eventually legal for any woman to end her preg-nancy whenever she and her doctor feel it's the best course" (Dirks & Relf, 2017, p. 75).

The CCS hoped that their status as religious leaders would empha-size the morality of their position and would insulate them from law enforcement. Indeed, in the United States members of the clergy have additional legal rights that would protect them from being compelled to give information to law enforcement. The 1958 Supreme Court decision *Mullen v. United States* "had established that clergy could not be compelled to reveal information received from parishioners as part of their confession." Though the CCS did take some legal precautions, like referring abortion patients to other states for care to confuse jurisdic-tions, CCS members were generally not afraid of being arrested (Dirks & Relf, 2017, p. 3). Some of them had already been arrested because of their work in the civil rights and anti-war movements (Dirks & Relf, 2017, p. 3). Ultimately, they didn't need to worry about arrest. No direct action was taken by law enforcement against the CCS. As one chief of detectives told a CCS organizer, "Look, we've got murders, rapes, and robberies where people get victimized. We're not interested in arresting people who help people. The only abortionists we're interested in are those who charge a thousand dollars and leave the woman dying" (Dirks & Relf, 2017, p. 76).

Though some may bristle at the idea of clergy working to access abortion care, for members of the CCS, this was a central part of their work as clergy. Activist and author D.A. Dirks and author Patricia Relf write, "many of the pastors we interviewed expressed the opinion that their pastoral counseling necessitated a commitment to compassionate care for women with unwanted pregnancies—their CCS work was simply a part of their job as ministers" (Dirks & Relf, 2017, p. 108). Reverend Howard Moody, one of the group's founders, argued that "the right to choose is a God-given right" and viewed "'the deification of the conceptus' as heret-ical, saying that birth was not a right but a gift from God and a woman" (Dirks & Relf, 2017, p. 105). Eventually, the CCS boasted chapters in thirty-eight states with more than three thousand members (Sherman & Mahone, 2024, p. 56). They helped an estimated 250,000 people access abortion care before abortion was legal in the United States (Sherman & Mahone, 2024, p. 56).

Ireland offers another example of the regulation of abortion. Until the recent repeal of the Eighth Amendment of the constitution in 2018, the criminalization of abortion resulted not only in concealed pregnancy and infanticide, but in an estimated 12,000 women every year, or more than 170,000 people since 1980, traveling to neighboring countries for legal abortion services, at great personal and financial expense. The most common destination was England, with many abortion health activist groups aiding in the facilitation of Irish women seeking abortion abroad (Duffy, 2020). While the number of individuals traveling abroad each year decreased consistently over time due to a higher level of contraceptive use among young adults (HSE Sexual Health & Crisis Pregnancy Programme, 2015), it is impossible to know the actual number of people who traveled from Ireland abroad for abortion, as these numbers reflect only those who gave an Irish address to health care providers abroad. Alternatively, women opted to self-manage abortion at home by ordering medicine online. This method of procuring an abortion was also illegal in Ireland, and while it is difficult to say exactly how many women sought abortion in this way, "the Health Products Regulatory Authority, working with Customs officials, seized 28 packages, containing 635 tablets, in 2011. By [2014] the numbers had almost doubled, to 1,017 tablets detained from 60 importations, suggesting that more pills are being imported" (Holland, 2014).

Abortion law in Ireland is shaped by its colonial past including the *1861 Offences Against the Person Act,* passed during the period of British colonial rule, which criminalized both those seeking as well as those performing abortion; the penalty being life imprisonment. This act continued past the formation of the Irish Free State and criminalization of abortion was deeply intertwined with Ireland's national identity as a Catholic country. This law has served as the basis of criminal law on abortion in Ireland, and was interpreted and amended throughout the years, creating a situation where abortion law in Ireland was ambiguous, restrictive, and unjust (Bakhru, 2017).

In 1983, in response to changing cultural and legal views on abortion starting in the 1970s, the Eighth Amendment (Article 40.3.3) to the Irish

Constitution was passed through referendum. As feminist legal scholars Enright et al. (2015) point out, the Eighth Amendment has a

> three-part provision relating to reproductive choice: first, a statement of a constitutionally protected foetal right to life to be protected and vindicated as far as practicable and with due regard to the equal right to life of the pregnant woman, a right to travel, and a right to receive information relating to reproductive choices. (The Legal Status Quo section)

Because the Eighth Amendment refers to the life of the unborn in particular, as opposed to abortion specifically, the entirety of a person's pregnancy is under its consideration. Should treatment for a life-threatening illness of the pregnant person be delayed if it could endanger the fetus? Can the pregnant person be subjected to unwanted medical treatment with the Eighth Amendment as justification? As in the fetal/maternal conflict, the Eighth Amendment to the Irish constitution situated the pregnant person and the fetus against each other (De Londras & Enright, 2018).

Over years of court cases and a patchwork of legislation created tremendous ambiguity for women and medical professionals in determining when an abortion might be lawful within Irish borders. While Irish law only allowed for abortion when the *life* of a woman was threatened there was no consideration for how the continuance of a pregnancy might affect the *health* of a woman. Several notable cases appear in the Irish context. In 1992, the case emerged of a young woman known as "X." "X" was refused the right to travel for an abortion after becoming pregnant as a result of rape even though her pregnancy was a risk to her life due to the threat of suicide. The X Case facilitated the clarification in the constitution of the right of Irish citizens to travel (not the right to abortion). 1997 saw the case of a 13-year-old girl known as "C" who faced obstacles in terminating a pregnancy that was an outcome of rape. She was taken into the care of the Eastern Health Board who petitioned on behalf of C for permission to travel abroad for an abortion. C's parents objected in the case A and B v.

Eastern Health Board and the judge ruled that because of the threat of suicide by C, she is entitled to an abortion. In 2007, a 17-year-old in the care of the state was refused right to travel to terminate an anencephalic pregnancy because she refused to say she was suicidal. This case is known as the D Case. The Health Service Executive requested that police detain her if she attempted to leave the country and that the Passport Office refuse to issue her a passport. In the D Case, the court ruled that D has the right to travel (not a right to an abortion) (IFPA, 2024).

As can be seen in each of these cases, restrictive regulations place the burden to access sometimes life-saving health care on the pregnant people themselves. Thus, ambiguity in Irish law has led to a disparity in access to sexual and reproductive health services: medical procedures that become accessible only to those who have the finances, knowledge, legal status, and time to travel outside Ireland for safe help with a crisis pregnancy. Unfortunately, there are many instances where the imperiled health of a pregnant woman can ultimately cause her death.

Access and criminalization

Even under broad legality, not everyone is able to access legal abortion. Some people are forced to give birth, while others seek out unregulated and sometimes illegal care. Take, for example, the case of Rosaura "Rosie" Jimenez, a daughter of migrant farm workers in Texas and a single mother. Rosie worked hard to support her family and to get an education. She had an abortion in 1975, and another in 1977, only a few years after *Roe* legalized abortion in the United States. Abortion could be expensive, but Rosie had government subsidized health insurance that paid for both procedures. Unfortunately, when Rosie needed a third abortion, a new federal provision, the Hyde Amendment, prevented her insurance from covering the abortion care. Unable to afford a legal abortion, Rosie sought an illegal abortion from an unlicensed provider and developed an infection. Without government assistance to access her newly acquired right to abortion, Rosie died from the illegal abortion in October 1977 (Sherman & Mahone, 2024).

Sometimes foreign policy can impact local realities for individuals seeking abortion. The infiltration of anti-abortion ideology from abroad can have real, material consequences for women and pregnant people's health. For example, the Global Gag Rule, also known as the Mexico City Policy, is a U.S. foreign policy created in 1984 and implemented through executive order that "deems non-US nongovernmental organizations (NGOs) ineligible for US government global health assistance if they provide, refer people for or promote abortion services—even if they use their own funding to do so" (Skuster et al., 2024). Over the past 40 years, the Global Gag Rule has been activated and deactivated multiple times by U.S. presidents based on their political party affiliation. When in place, the Global Gag Rule ensures that NGOs outside the United States receiving any U.S. global health funds must stop providing or referring clients to any abortion related services or advocacy, even if the money for these activities is their own non-U.S. based funds and abortion provision, education, and advocacy is legal in that country. The negative results of the policy originating in the United States are far-reaching and significant for countries around the world. In addition to loss of critical funds globally for abortion services and counseling, other services provided by NGOs like HIV/AIDS support, contraception, and prenatal care are also collaterally impacted.

The Global Gag Rule has objectively harmed people's health. There is no evidence of any positive outcomes from its implementation. People seeking care have decreased access to abortion and contraception information and services. Health care providers experience intrusion into their relationships with their patients and experience pressure and discouragement from providing the full range of care. Public health systems are impacted by reduced community health workers and outreach, and must spend additional time searching for alternative funds (Guttmacher Institute, n.d.). In a report by the Guttmacher Institute, Skuster et al. (2020) detail the findings of their multi-year study on the impact of the Global Gag Rule in Uganda and Ethiopia. In both countries, which have differing legal provisions for abortion, the Global Gag Rule disrupted and reversed progress on access to contraception, reproductive health outcomes, family planning and spacing of children, and bodily autonomy overall. The Gag Rule hastened a closing of clinics and mobile outreach services that provided a variety of services including prenatal care. There was a loss of service integration and a weakened advocacy environment. Because NGOs that are impacted by the Global Gag Rule often support national health programs, when the NGO loses funding it sends a ripple effect impacting the entire public health system. In fact, the study found that during the period the gag rule was in effect in Uganda, which has very stringent abortion laws, the number of women seeking postabortion care from complications due to clandestine abortion increased after contraception education and distribution was disrupted.

The criminalization of abortion is related to other forms of pregnancy criminalization. For example, decades before *Roe* was overturned, pregnant people in the United States were subject to investigation and state intervention for outcomes of their pregnancies. This was based on an understanding that fertilized eggs, embryos, and fetuses were legal persons being abused by those who gestate them, or that pregnant people were damaging their pregnancies and would give birth to expensive, needy infants that would grow into dangerously criminal and antisocial adults (Flavin, 2008; Flavin & Paltrow, 2010; Goodwin, 2020; Howard, 2024; Mohapatra, 2011; Murphy & Rosenbaum, 1999; Paltrow & Flavin, 2013; Roberts, 1990; Roberts, 1992; Roberts, 1996; Roberts, 2014).

Even when states ban abortion, people find ways to resist those restrictions. Banning abortion doesn't make it go away. For example, despite the increasing illegality of abortion in the United States—with fifteen states banning nearly all abortions—the number of abortions performed in the country is actually increasing (Society of Family Planning, 2025). Travel from states with bans to states without bans, and the proliferation of the abortion pill, are allowing people to circumvent the law (Maddow-Zimet & Gibson, 2024). These efforts, however, do not eliminate the risks created by pregnancy criminalization.

Sometimes, though, attempts to maneuver around the law are unsuccessful. In addition to not being able to access care, people have been prosecuted or penalized under pregnancy-related laws. People like Purvi

Patel, who are accused of causing miscarriage or stillbirth and charged with feticide; people like Brittany Watts, who are charged because of what they did after their miscarriage; people like Amanda Kimbrough, who test positive for drugs during birth and are charged with child abuse; and people who are deemed to have otherwise threatened their pregnancies (for example, by attempting suicide, fleeing from law enforcement, refusing to submit to medical procedures) can all result in criminal prosecution (Howard, 2023, 2024; Redden, 2016).

As Grace Howard wrote in *The Pregnancy Police: Conceiving Crime, Arresting Personhood*, "the criminal prosecution of pregnant people for crimes against the fertilized eggs, embryos, and fetuses that they carry relies on a legal understanding that pregnant people are legally distinct from and enjoy fewer rights than other similarly situated nonpregnant people" (2024, p. 3). In these cases, pregnancy itself becomes the basis for legal vulnerability, making these pregnancy-related charges a kind of status crime (Ocen, 2017). State regulation of abortion determines which bodies are considered valuable and fully human, and which are not.

Conclusion

Abortion is not only a widespread reproductive reality but also a deeply political and social issue that reflects broader global inequities in power, gender, race, class, and bodily autonomy. This chapter has traced how access to abortion is shaped by historical and contemporary forms of regulation, ranging from colonial-era criminal codes and eugenics to modern human rights frameworks and LGBTQ+ advocacy. Across the world, individuals seek abortion for overlapping and often urgent reasons— economic insecurity, relationship instability, health concerns, and aspirations for education or stability. And yet, restrictive laws, social stigma, religious conservatism, and disinformation campaigns continue to undermine access, safety, and dignity. While international organizations increasingly recognize abortion as essential to public health and gender equality, legal frameworks remain uneven, with devastating consequences for marginalized populations. The persistence of unsafe abortion, despite advances in medical technology and human rights law, exposes the fatal cost of criminalization and the urgent need for inclusive, culturally responsive care.

Abortion cannot be understood in isolation; it is linked to the history of regulating gendered bodies, from reproductive coercion to pregnancy criminalization. While countries like Ireland demonstrate the power of grassroots activism and legal reform, global forces, including U.S. foreign policy, continue to shape what services are available and to whom. To ensure reproductive justice, advocates, scholars, and policymakers must reframe abortion not as a personal failing or moral crisis, but as a structural issue of equity, health, and freedom. A truly just world is one in which all people can make informed, supported, and autonomous decisions about their reproductive lives.

4

what should we do about abortion?

Introduction

This chapter argues that we must reframe the current discourse around abortion and employ a human rights-based framework in order to address the complexities, range, and nuance of abortion issues. It highlights the need to move beyond neoliberal conceptions of choice as it pertains to abortion and the necessity to facilitate coalition building and collaborative work between social movements. It concludes with three case studies in which activists and organizers were able to use an intersectional, human rights-based framework to advocate for change to abortion policy and practice. These case studies illustrate the social change that can occur when an intersectional, human rights-based framework is applied to the issue of abortion.

What is reproductive justice?

Reproductive justice is an intersectional, human rights-based framework that is focused on shifting power by putting the voices and experiences of those on the margins at the center of analysis. It "makes the link between the individual and community, addresses government and corporate responsibility, fights all forms of population control (eugenics)" (Ross et al., 2017, p. 19). It is built on principles of sexual freedom and bodily autonomy. Reproductive justice underscores the importance of recognizing the historical, legal, and economic contexts—in other words the social context—in which women and pregnant people's lives are lived, when understanding their reproductive lives. It also approaches reproductive health matters intersectionally, by recognizing the multiple forms of oppression that intersect and overlap to shape one's experiences, and therefore the need to work collectively through alliances and coalitions for change (Crenshaw, 2017). It acknowledges that regardless of how various institutions, like government, religion, or medicine, regulate their bodies, women and people with the capacity for pregnancy always have and will continue to shape their reproductive destinies to the extent they can.

The Reproductive Justice framework, created in 1994, is a radical articulation of reproductive freedom stemming from the experiences of Black women in the United States. It is a transnational framework that offers a holistic model of theory and activism focused on three principles: (1) the right not to have children; (2) the right to have children; and (3) the right to parent children one already has. Reproductive justice scholars Ross and Solinger (2017) state, "At the heart of reproductive justice is this claim: all fertile persons and persons who reproduce and become parents require a safe and dignified context for these most fundamental human experiences" (p. 9). It points to the sense that "our collective sexual consciousness has been warped by misogyny, slavery, and colonialism" (Ross et al., 2017, p. 175). There is not a single individual or community that remains untouched by histories of colonization and global capitalism and the resulting discrimination and oppression.

These factors underpin rules and regulations that shape the reproductive lives of people with the capacity for pregnancy in varying places across geography, time, and social location. In this way the reproductive justice framework draws on intersectionality to understand a person or community's reproductive health experiences. Underdevelopment, poverty, and the exploitation of natural resources are linked to reproduction, shape reproductive experiences, and inform reproductive politics. Reproductive justice brings to light the ways that systems of oppression like white supremacy, sexism, and capitalism work together over time in determining the worth, utility, and value of certain bodies over others, and the ways in which children can become a kind of currency in this system (Briggs, 2017; Ross, 2020; Ross et al., 2016; Ross & Solinger, 2017). It is a framework that is wide reaching and illuminating when we understand it in a broad and encompassing context.

Reproductive histories vary globally. Because of race, economic status, or other markers of identity, some may struggle to control their fertility through access to contraception and abortion while others struggle to raise the children they have. When women are singularly bound by and to their roles as mothers and caregivers they cannot be full participants in society. But this sentiment isn't restricted to abortion only. Laws that decriminalize contraception and abortion, adequate funding for reproductive health care services and clinics, freedom from sexual coercion, violence, or forced sterilization, a work environment free from toxic chemicals linked to miscarriage, or access to clean air and water to raise healthy children are all connected and all part of a reproductive justice agenda. At its heart, the reproductive justice framework claims that all people must have bodily autonomy and determine their reproductive destinies free from coercion, whether that be coerced sex and reproduction or coerced suppression or termination of fertility (Ross & Solinger 2017, p. 17).

The material resources needed to ensure such a context, like housing, food, economic means, clear water and air, or freedom from discrimination and violence are themselves also conditions of the realization of reproductive justice within a human rights framework. Feminist scholars Correa and Petchesky (1994) refer to these resources as *enabling conditions.* They say, "These conditions constitute the foundation of reproductive and sexual rights and are what feminists mean when they speak of women's 'empowerment.' [...] Such enabling conditions, or social rights, are integral to reproductive and sexual rights and directly entail the responsibility of states and mediating institutions for the implementation" (p. 112). Notions of enabling conditions move beyond the idea of personal choice and public action as separate. In fact, racism, sexism, xenophobia, poverty, lack of access to health care services or education all directly impact the power and resources one has to make the decisions one wants to make about their body. Inherent in the actualization of enabling conditions is the idea that personal well-being and the social good are connected. The battle for reproductive justice is the battle for social justice and equity in all realms of life.

The idea of reproductive justice grows in tandem with an international women's health movement which emerged as a force around the world committed to empowering women to control their own fertility and sexuality with minimal risk and maximum decision-making power. With regard to such an ideological basis for political action, Petchesky states that

> informing every aspect of this ethical core is a realization drawn from
> women's everyday experience: that, particularly for women, all
> human rights—rights to political and bodily self-determination,
> health and development—have both personal and social dimensions,
> and these are integrally connected. (Petchesky, 2003, p. 8)

Indeed, the agenda feminist activists and scholars focusing on reproductive justice are advocating for is rooted in a connection made between the everyday lived experiences and the politics surrounding bodily self-determination. While the term reproductive justice stems specifically from the work and lives of African American women, it is a theory, strategy, and practice that can apply to everyone and is deeply intertwined with work already being done by feminist groups around the world.

The limits of choice

Our bodies carry social and political meaning. Rules and regulations made around and carried out on the body signify a host of ideas concerning which bodies matter, which individuals and communities are valuable, and which families are legible. For these reasons, configuring reproductive health matters in general and abortion specifically within a framework of "choice" does not take into account all the social, political, and economic factors that influence the ways that people with the capacity for pregnancy make reproductive health related decisions.

Perceptions of reproductive choice rely on capitalist imaginings of choice-making. Choice treats reproductive health and reproductive health services, such as abortion, as commodities and shapes the ways individuals and communities perceive and negotiate their sexual and reproductive freedoms. The choice framework, informed by capitalist ideology, fails to enforce the idea that women have inherent rights, but rather implies the idea that women should be able to make choices if they can afford them or if they are deemed legitimate choice-makers (Smith, 2005). From such a perspective, it is not clear what should happen to those individuals and communities who have limited access to the free market or who are marked as incapable or unworthy of making a choice. They are deemed "illegitimate" choice makers, because they do not rely on the market to exercise their "rights" or fit into a "brand culture" of choice. People with the capacity for pregnancy who are disabled, asylum-seeking, refugees, incarcerated, living in poverty, members of racial or ethnic minorities, or who are dependent on the state in some way through government subsidies for housing or food often lack power and resources to make their choices come to fruition—whether that choice is to limit the number and spacing of their children or to raise the children they want or already have.

For example, during times of social, political, economic, or climate crisis people with the capacity for pregnancy can become displaced internally or relocated to a refugee camp. Conditions may be harsh and inhospitable. It is not uncommon that, in times of conflict, medical facilities are destroyed, creating supply shortages for clinics—from items as common as soap to basic surgical instruments for birth. Crises, natural, and manufactured, make the need for reproductive health care more pronounced and more difficult to access. Social, political, economic, and climate crises heighten already serious risks for people with the capacity for pregnancy.

Sexual violence in conflict zones results in forced pregnancy, forced marriage, forced prostitution, and sexual slavery, among other harms. Still, a 2013 global survey of sexual and reproductive health provision in humanitarian settings showed that safe abortion was unavailable in every facility in the study (Fetters et al., 2020). "Premature deliveries, miscarriages brought on by trauma and unsafe abortions resulting from unwanted pregnancies are all linked to crisis situations—and all require medical treatment" (UNFPA, 2001, p. 6). There is an assumption that those experiencing displacement and refugee status have no need for abortion services, that humanitarian aid doesn't and shouldn't include abortion services, and abortion is too complicated during acute emergencies (Fetters et al., 2020). The need for abortion services is crucial among refugees and internally displaced people during crises where 60% of preventable maternal mortality occurs.

Because women are seen as reproducing both biologically and socially in their roles as raising children, Indigenous women's fertility remains the primary targets of forced sterilization campaigns. Cases in the United States, Canada, Peru, and Australia, to name a few, show instances of forced family separation, abuse of power by healthcare professionals, the undermining of consent processes, and coercion to enforce involuntary sterilization, as we discussed in Chapter 2. We can see repeated use of coercive sterilization and child removal on Indigenous women as a means of population control, cultural genocide, and ensuring a racial hierarchy in order to implement and the sustain occupation of land and extraction of resources (Rowlands et al., 2025).

In contexts such as these—displacement, being subjected to sexual violence, miscarriage as a result of trauma—what constitutes choice-making? If one's ability to reproduce has been taken away involuntarily because they have been deemed less "civilized" or less intelligent, or a drain on society, how does one enact the choices they want to make about their bodies? This can be said of many intersections of identity which have been used to justify curtailing agency and reproductive capacity of individuals and communities. Even if a person retains their reproductive capacity but is forced to make a decision based on factors like their health status, insecurity due to war or natural disaster, pressure from cultural or religious traditions, or status as a refugee, is that decision a choice (Chrisler, 2012)? As Ross and Solinger state, "Individual choices have only been as capacious and empowering as the resources any woman can turn to in her community" (Ross & Solinger 2017, p. 16).

Thinking beyond choice to justice centers bodily autonomy and control over one's reproductive destiny within a human rights framework. If rights cannot be realized, they are only symbolic. The reproductive justice framework acknowledges the systematic and institutionalized barriers that limit one's ability to engage in choice making in real and material ways and argues those barriers must be addressed in order to have full sexual and reproductive freedom.

Engagement with human rights

One aspect of the reproductive justice framework that makes it so potentially transformative is its explicit engagement with a human rights framework. The Human Rights framework posits that there is an inherent dignity in human existence and that all people have inalienable rights. These rights serve as a foundation for freedom, justice, and peace in the world (United Nations, 1948). The United Nations' Universal Declaration of Human Rights (UDHR), along with many subsequent conventions and treaties, outline and proclaim that societies have a responsibility to protect the freedom and dignity of human beings. As Ross and Solinger (2017) state, "Reproductive justice is the application of the concept of inter-sectionality to reproductive politics in order to achieve human rights" (p. 79). Using a human rights framework has often been done in organizing for reproductive freedom in the Global South. Human rights discourse has been used by many feminist movements transnationally to invoke an internationally recognized set of tenants with which to hold governments to account (Cook et al., 2014; Luna, 2020; Rebouché, 2017; Ross, 2020). The human rights frame "encourages marginalized people to work collectively to challenge inequality under the rubric of gaining wide human rights that go beyond the limited rights supported by any particular government" (Luna, 2020, p. 66).

The human rights framework is a moral, political, and legal structure and gives us a method for determining whose and which needs should take precedence. It assigns obligations to specific parties for fulfilling those needs and empowers those whose needs are at stake to speak for themselves. To enact human rights means not only prohibiting reproductive violence and discrimination but actively protecting individuals from harm by promoting safe sexual relationships and addressing sexual violence. This means that governments and other entities, like medical, educational, or civil society institutions, must commit to actively protecting individuals from sexual harm and promoting safe sexual relationships. While almost all governments have laws and policies against sexual violence, the extent and implementation of such laws is flawed and limited, and sexual violence continues to occur at alarming rates. Importantly, the promotion of safe, consensual sexual relationships, bodily autonomy, and reproductive freedom both inside and outside sanctioned marriage must be seen as a legitimate subject of public education and expenditure:

> Based on such established human rights principles, feminists affirm that women's health, pleasure, and empowerment must be treated as ends in themselves and not merely as means towards other social goals—for example, reducing population numbers, producing more healthy babies, or helping to create and expand markets and cheap labor pools. (Murray, 2008, p. 9)

Supporting sexual and reproductive health as human rights means investing in the prevention of discrimination and abuse, and in the promotion of safe sexual relationships by governments and civil society. Therefore, bodily integrity must be central to public and economic policies, public services, and education. This in turn will promote safe, consensual sexual relationships, supported by governments, health departments, and NGOs that provide information and services (Berer, 2004). Applying the human rights framework to reproduction begs the question: do pregnant people get to be fully human? When a person becomes pregnant, have they transformed into a legal non-person, or a less-human entity for the duration of the pregnancy?

The Jane Collective: United States

In the United States before *Roe v. Wade*, there were groups dedicated to helping people access safe, extra-legal abortion care. The Abortion Service, better known today as the Jane Collective, was a group of women in Chicago with no formal medical training, who provided thousands of safe abortions in Chicago from 1964 to 1973 (Kaplan, 2019). What had first started in 1964 as one university student making sporadic referrals to safe abortion providers had by 1969 grown into an organized group whose aim was helping the women of Chicago take their bodies and their destinies into their own hands and out of medical and legal authority.

Jane grew out of the civil rights, anti-Vietnam War, and women's liberation movements. Heather Booth, then a student at the University of Chicago, got a phone call from a friend who was trying to find a safe way for her sister to have an abortion (Kaplan, 2019). As more requests for abortion referrals came through, Heather adopted the pseudonym "Jane" to protect her anonymity (Kaplan, 2019). If somebody called her dorm room looking for an abortion, they would ask for Jane. By the time she graduated, Heather had helped more than one hundred women access abortions (King, 1993).

Eventually, as other members got involved and the group grew, new strategies were used. They moved out of the dorm room and established a rotating pair of office locations. The first, known as "the front" was where people seeking abortion care came for holistic, feminist abortion counseling—an opportunity to talk through their situation, share concerns, fears, hopes, and to discuss the procedure itself. Jane provided food, childcare, and a safe, comforting place for people to wait before, and during, abortion appointments. The second location, known as "the place," is where abortions were performed, on beds with clean linens, in comfortably decorated, homey apartments.

At first, Jane vetted abortion providers. Not every abortion provider was competent or safe. Some would leave patients bleeding out or with infections. Some charged exploitative prices. Some were drunk. Some demanded sexual favors before the procedure would be offered. Jane worked to find providers who could provide medically and emotionally safe abortions. One of Jane's abortion providers, a man named Mike, flew from California to Chicago on the weekends to provide abortions (Fischer, 2016). By 1971, this changed. During an abortion procedure, Mike handed his medical instruments over to a Jane named Jody, asking if she wanted "to just see what it feels like" to complete the abortion (King, 1993). This was a pivotal moment for The Abortion Service. Some of the Janes started learning how to do abortions themselves.

The Janes had hired Mike based on an understanding that he was a physician—an obstetrician. This, however, was incorrect. Mike was not a doctor. He had no formal medical training. And yet, he was capable of providing safe abortions. If he could do it, why couldn't the Janes do it? Afterall, abortion hadn't always been in the domain of physicians and medical care. If they were going to challenge the legitimacy of the law, why not challenge medical authority as well? This would enable The Abortion Service to provide more abortions—no longer limited to what one pair of hands could do over a weekend. The Janes had been paying Mike for his services. Without that expense, they could lower the price of each abortion. Abortion providers for The Service needed to be skilled, even more-so than physicians. Mistakes and complications are a normal part of medical practice and would be anticipated in formal medical settings, but the Janes were working illegally. Any complication could result in investigation, prosecution, and the entire operation being shut down. By 1971, the Janes were providing abortions on their own.

The Abortion Service acquired supplies through multiple means. King writes, "sympathetic doctors and nurses made supplies or instruments available to Jane. Some pharmacists supplied drugs and disposable items" (1993). Some Janes used their own prescriptions to acquire medications for patients (King, 1993). On the advice of another abortion provider, a few members "merely walked into a surgical supply house, with an air of confidence, and made an order" (King, 1993). Members of The Abortion Service also needed ways to dispose of the products of conception. For procedures performed earlier in pregnancy, they would flush the tissue down the toilet. For more developed pregnancies, other methods were necessary. Sometimes, men who were friends, husbands, or lovers of Janes would assume this task. Apparently, they often used supermarket dumpsters at night (Bart, 1987).

Many Jane members anticipated being arrested for this work, and were somewhat baffled when it didn't happen (King, 1993). They were prepared for a raid, shredding or chewing and eating paper records with the names and identification of patients (King, 1993). Neighborhood police *knew* about Jane. King writes, "Reportedly, neighborhood policemen were aware of Jane, and at times they greeted participants on the street with 'Hi, Jane'" (1993 p. 86). Eventually they learned that the police didn't disturb them before because they saw the Janes as providing a necessary service for them—for policewomen, for their wives, mistresses, girlfriends, and daughters. As Bart writes, "Jane did not leave bleeding bodies in motels for the police to deal with" the way other illegal abortion providers did. By 1972, Jane was providing around 100 abortions a week (Bart 1987, p. 346).

However, On May 3, 1972, the Chicago police raided The Service, and arrests were made. The police had been tipped off by a woman trying to stop her sister-in-law from having an abortion (Bart, 1987; Sherman & Mahoney, 2024). Apparently, the Janes had already completed 23 abortions that day, and at the time of the raid, three women were in recovery from their procedures (King, 1993; Sherman & Mahoney, 2024). First, the police raided The Place. Then, the police raided The Front, where seven women were still waiting for their procedures (Sherman & Mahoney, 2024). On the way to the police station, "the arrested Jane members ripped up their intake notecards and ate the pieces of paper [...] to protect the identities of the women they served, and they flushed their money to prevent the police from taking it" (Sherman & Mahoney, 2024, p. 67).

Despite the arrests, The Abortion Service continued their work. The women who hadn't gotten their abortions on the day of the raid were not abandoned. The Abortion Service raised money to send the women to Washington D.C. or New York City, where abortion was legal. All of them still got their abortions (Sherman & Mahoney, 2024, p. 68). While not all Janes continued their work with The Abortion Service, others "doubled down on their work as the calls for services increased" (Sherman & Mahoney, 2024, p. 68). One Jane said that "those who stayed changed their daily routines, assumed that they were being followed, and made changes to tighten up security measures."

Seven Jane members were taken into custody and held in jail for a night. They faced charges of conspiracy to commit abortion, and up to 110 years in prison (Sherman & Mahoney, 2024, p. 67). The "Abortion 7" hired lawyer Jo-Anne Wolfson to represent them (Sherman & Mahoney, 2024, p. 69). Sherman and Mahoney write, "Wolfson learned that the police raid was a bit of a mistake and that if certain higher-ups in the Chicago Police Department hadn't been on vacation that week it probably would have never happened" (2024, p. 69). Apparently, the raid had taken place under the direction of a new police captain who didn't know about the "hands off" policy.

The Abortion 7 were released from jail on bonds equivalent to $19,000 in 2024 U.S. dollars (Sherman & Mahoney, 2024, p. 69). When *Roe* made abortion legal nationwide in January 1973, the charges against the Abortion 7 were dropped. Jane disbanded soon after. During the final years of criminalization, between 1969 and 1973, Jane provided around 11,000 abortions (Bart, 1987).

As the United States settles into its latest period of abortion criminalization, some of us look back at Jane and wonder if it's time for a revival. However, the reality is, Jane is already here. We may not know all of them by name, as the law may necessitate discretion, but groups that help people access abortion care exist all over the world—who recognize that while we work toward changing the law, we also help our communities meet their needs. Practical support groups for abortion and abortion funds help find safe providers, arrange transportation and lodging accommodations, and fund abortion care. Networks of physicians, pharmacists, advocates, and others, have been able to get abortion pills into the hands of people that need them, regardless of their legality. Acompañamiento, or accompaniment, a practice that grew out of Latin American feminist abortion rights groups, helps guide people through safely self-managing abortions.

Repeal the 8th campaign: Ireland

The Eighth Amendment of the Irish Constitution criminalized abortion by regarding the right to life of the unborn as equal to the right to life of the mother. *Repeal the 8th* was a national grassroots campaign that engaged with feminism, exercised embodied politics, and human rights frameworks to fight for reproductive freedom by repealing the Eighth Amendment of the Irish constitution.

As discussed in Chapter 2, Article 40.3.3 (the Eighth Amendment of the Irish Constitution) was passed in 1983 in response to progressive change in attitudes towards cultural and social issues. The most restrictive aspects of Article 40.3.3 stated that: The State acknowledges the right to life of the unborn and, with due regard to the equal right to life of the mother, guarantees in its laws to respect, and, as far as practicable, by its laws to defend and vindicate that right (Enright et al., 2015, The Legal Status Quo section).

The anticipated consequences of such ambiguity in Irish law and the delay of the State to clarify its own constitution came to a head in October 2012. Savita Halappanavar, an immigrant to Ireland of Indian descent, died due to complications resulting from her refused request for an abortion in an Irish hospital. Although the amniotic sac had broken, she was miscarrying, and her fetus was not viable outside the womb, Savita and her husband, Praveen, were told that because fetal heartbeat was still present and because "Ireland is a Catholic country" an abortion was not possible. The result of the mismanagement of Halappanavar's case led to her death from septicemia and *E. coli*, causing shock to the body and multi-organ failure (Lentin, 2013, p. 130).

Savita Halappanavar's death sent a tremor through the nation and within days thousands protested on the streets of Dublin in remembrance of her and to demand change in the country's abortion laws (Fallon, 2012). Investigation into Halappanavar's death found "a failure in the provision of the most basic elements of patient care" (Health Information and Quality Authority, 2013, para. 2). Furthermore, "interpretation of the law related to lawful termination in Ireland is considered to have been a material contributory factor" in her death (Waterfield, 2013, para. 3). The case of Savita Halappanavar made apparent that Irish abortion laws' lack of clarity in the distinction between the *life* and the *health* of the mother creates an unsustainable situation that puts women's lives at risk. It also made transparent, yet again, that the Irish state's long-standing reliance on neighboring countries, such as the UK, to access abortion services will inevitably fail to protect women who are not able, for whatever reasons, to travel without restriction. Furthermore, the circumstances of Halappanavar's death reinforce a history of indignity that women in Ireland have endured, time and again, when facing a crisis pregnancy.

The death of Halappanavar was a significant factor in a shifting of public attitudes and political mobilization to challenge the stringent and dysfunctional abortion laws in Ireland. Additionally, at the same time, Ireland's abortion laws were being publicly criticized by several United Nations monitoring bodies for violations of human rights (Kennedy, 2018). In one instance in 2005 along the journey toward reproductive freedom, the restrictive and ambiguous legal circumstances of abortion in Ireland led three women to take a case against Ireland to the European Court of Human Rights. An oral hearing of the case was delivered before the Grand Chamber of 17 Judges on December 9, 2009. The women, known as A, B and C to protect their confidentiality, argued that Ireland breached their human rights under Articles 2 (Right to Life), 3 (Prohibition of Torture), 8 (Right to Respect for Family and Private Life), and 14 (Prohibition of Discrimination) of the European Convention on Human Rights. In 2010 the European Court of Human Rights ruled that applicant C's human rights were violated under Article 8 of the European Court of

Human Rights by the Irish State in its failure to implement existing constitutional law (Irish Family Planning Association, n.d.; Kolbert & Kay, 2021). In 2010, the European Court of Human Rights ruled in a case called ABC, where three women challenged Irish abortion law, that ambiguity in Irish abortion law violates a woman's rights under Article 8 of the European Convention on Human Rights. In 2013, the Irish government passed the Protection of Life During Pregnancy Act (PLDPA), which created a differentiation between a physical threat to life and a threat to life due to mental health risk (suicide). Irish feminist scholar Kennedy (2018) highlights the highly dysfunctional nature of this act. She states,

> Where the threat arises because of risk of suicide, three doctors—an obstetrician and two psychiatrists—must agree that the woman's life is at risk. If this panel did not agree, she could be referred to a further panel of three doctors. This created a situation whereby a suicidal, pregnant woman could potentially face a situation of being questioned by up to six doctors before accessing abortion (p. 25)

The consequence of such cumbersome legislation came to fruition in 2014 when a migrant woman with limited English speaking skills who became pregnant as a result of rape was denied an abortion and became suicidal. Her request continued to be ignored and she consequently went on a hunger strike. In response the High Court issued an order to force feed her. She was eventually "convinced" into continuing her pregnancy until the fetus was viable at which point she was induced (Kennedy, 2018, p. 25). As Tella (2023) states

> The activism in the years following Savita Halappanavar's death were razor focused on the issue of reproductive rights and the right to health and life, and the issue of violation of basic human rights... The rhetoric of the abortion debate shifted from one of preserving the nation to that of the state's duty to provide healthcare and protect a woman's right to health that was part of her right to life. (p. 73)

As a result of this compilation of human rights violations, pressure and grassroots mobilization mounted. The Abortion Rights Campaign formed in 2012 and called for safe, free, legal abortion in Ireland. In 2013, a coalition of individuals and organizations formed the Coalition to Repeal the Eighth Amendment. In 2016 the group Strike for Repeal organized a public action around International Women's Day that resulted in the strike of thousands of people, walking out of schools and universities, shutting down the city centre of Dublin. The Irish government was feeling the growing pressure to respond. In 2016 the Citizens' Assembly was formed to provide recommendations on abortion to the government. After much deliberation and hearing from women across Ireland, the Citizens' Assembly recommended that Article 40.3.3 of the Irish Constitution be removed. As Kennedy (2018) states, "This was the first time in the history of the State's engagement with the issue of abortion that women's voices and direct experiences were publicly heard and listened to" (p. 26). In January of 2018 the government announced that a referendum would be held in the summer of that year. While previous referendums on the right to travel and the right to information were supported, these issues were adjacent to the issue of abortion but did not address it directly.

Together for Yes, a coalition of more than 70 groups and organizations from across civil society, mobilized the referendum effort. The campaign platform was made of

> dozens of member organizations including those formed specifically to campaign for a yes vote, longer-standing advocacy groups, trades unions, and NGOs. The Campaign Platform was the most representative part of the campaign infrastructure, and included groups that advocate for the (general and reproductive) rights of migrant and ethnic minority persons in Ireland (such as MERJ, AkiDwA, National Traveller Women's Forum, and the Anti-Racism Network), and those that advocate for trans (reproductive and general) rights in Ireland. (such as Transgender Equality Network Ireland, NXF National LGBT Federation, and LGBT+ for Choice) (DeLondres, 2020, chapter 6)

In 2018, the Eighth Amendment to the Irish constitution was repealed with 66.4% of the vote. The subsequent Health Act 2018 allowed for abortion up to 12 weeks to be legally available and permissible upon medical grounds after 12 weeks (Tella, 2023).

In the post referendum period there is much discussion of the need to ensure that abortion access for women and pregnant people living in Ireland is accessible. As DeLondres (2020) states, in the end,

> the law that emerged from these victories left many behind, especially those for whom multiple marginalities intersect to make domestic abortion travel difficult if not impossible, those whose gender presentation does not match a 'female' marker assigned at birth, those with reduced access (for mobility or other reasons) to transportation and healthcare, and those racialised by both the containment practices of Irish refugee and immigration law and the persistent partition of the island of Ireland (chapter 6).

Discussion, debate, and organizing work continues to ensure to make sure abortion is fully accessible in Ireland.

Although the results of the referendum fell short of all of the expectations of the coalition of organizing groups, the efforts to reframe abortion through Reproductive Justice based on human rights and collective action cannot be disregarded. Moving beyond neoliberal "choice" discourses enables broader inclusivity and equity, that conversation and mobilization continues. For these reasons the Ireland's *Repeal the 8th* campaign provides us with an example of the transformative power of grassroots, rights-based organizing, affirming the global need to center dignity, access, and justice in reproductive struggles. The *Repeal the 8th* campaign in Ireland exemplifies a reproductive justice framework by centering the lived experiences of marginalized people and framing abortion not simply as a matter of choice, but as a human rights issue rooted in dignity, equity, and structural change. While traditional pro-choice narratives often focus on individual autonomy, the *Repeal* campaign broadened the conversation to include the social, legal, and economic conditions that shape reproductive freedom—especially for migrants, asylum seekers, disabled people, and those living in poverty.

Rather than treating abortion as an isolated issue, activists connected it to broader struggles for healthcare access, freedom from state violence, and the right to parent without fear or coercion. The movement's grass-roots nature and diverse coalition—including LGBTQ+ groups, disability rights advocates, and migrant-led organizations—embodied the intersectional vision at the heart of reproductive justice. Tactics like *Strike for Repeal* and testimonies shared in the Citizens' Assembly placed the voices of those most affected at the center, highlighting the systemic failures of the Irish state to uphold reproductive rights and health.

Although legal reform through the 2018 referendum marked a major victory, reproductive justice advocates continue to emphasize that access remains unequal. As De Londras (2018) points out, legal change alone does not guarantee meaningful access for all. The *Repeal* campaign's lasting legacy lies in its transformative approach—shifting public discourse, challenging stigma, and building a foundation for continued struggles toward full reproductive justice in Ireland.

Joint action for reproductive justice (Moduleul wihan nagtaejoe pyeji haengdong, 모두를 위한 낙태죄 폐지 행동): South Korea

The final case study shows parallels between Romania's Decree 770 and South Korea's hypocritical stance on abortion. It examines the work of the Korean feminist coalition Joint Action for Reproductive Justice. Through centering human rights, economic gender equity, and democratic ideals, feminist activists lobbied for change in cultural attitudes around sexual and reproductive health matters as well as to the law. South Korea's stance on abortion can be characterized as state intervention in women's reproductive capacities for the sake of national interest. In 1953, The Criminal Act outlawed abortion on any grounds. However, in the decades following the Korean War, 1950–1990, anti-natalism and population control were widely promoted as a reduction in the national fertility rate was necessary to receive international aid for economic development.

Governments have attempted to grow or to shrink the size of their populations, depending on their needs. Beginning in the 1960s, there has been concern about the growing global population, and population growth in developing countries in particular. Biologist Paul Ehrlich, whose book *The Population Bomb* compared human population growth to metastasizing cancer and endorsed mandatory birth regulation and the addition of sterilants to food and water supplies, also shaped public discourse on reproductive control. The growing global population was blamed for poverty, unemployment, environmental devastation, famine, and genocide. This perspective, however, should be challenged. Much of the drive to slow or reverse population growth in developing countries came from developed countries, who themselves are responsible for the vast majority of environmental devastation and resource usage. The problem isn't humanity, but capitalism, which requires constant exponential growth and unlimited use of environmental resources. Indeed, this critique allows us to examine some of the other motivations for trying to shape global populations.

Population control measures in developing countries can be an internal governmental strategy to achieve development goals, but population control has also been funded and imposed by developed nations and organizations like the World Bank and the Population Council for their own political purposes. For example, during the Cold War, there was concern that rapid population growth in the "third world" would lead to unrest, revolution, and the spread of communism.

Underpopulation can also result in government concern: will there be enough soldiers, workers, and consumers to fulfill government plans? Will there be enough young people to take care of the elderly? This can be particularly troubling when a government is attempting to curate a national image: an ideal citizen. Attempting to increase the birth rate is referred to as pronatalism. This can be accomplished by incentivizing birth through access to medical care; paid time off work; accessible child-care; tax incentives; birth bonus payments; and subsidized fertility treatment and by exposing the population to state propaganda idealizing motherhood and framing motherhood as a national duty; and even by awarding government honors to people who birth a large number of children. As we discussed in Chapter 1, governments have also attempted to increase the birth rate more coercively by eliminating contraception and abortion.

Romania provides a particularly compelling example. By the 1960s, Romania was attempting to eliminate the Russian influence on Romanian life and culture. Under the leadership of Nicolae Ceausescu, Romania continued a project of intense industrialization, and worked to cultivate an idealized national image. But in the 1960s, the Romanian birth rate began to decline. To accomplish its economic goals, the Romanian government wanted to increase the population from 23 to 30 million. In 1966, Ceausescu signed Decree 770, which criminalized abortion and functionally banned contraceptives. The birth rate doubled in a single year. Members of the secret police and prosecutors were stationed at hospitals to ensure doctors weren't providing abortions and to investigate suspected abortions. Women were required to submit to gynecologic examinations every month, and doctors were supposed to report pregnancies to the government. A suspected abortion could result in interrogation, threats of arrest, withholding of medical treatment, and even beatings, in an attempt to get the patient to report whoever had helped her abort her pregnancy.

Couples were expected to have five children, and fertile adults without children were required to pay a 30% celibacy tax. Pregnant girls were removed from school. Unmarried women who gave birth routinely lost custody of their children. Unmarried women didn't fit into the image the Romanian state was trying to cultivate and were not trusted to raise good Romanian citizens. Orphanages were flooded with children who had been taken from their mothers, with children whose families could not support them, and with children whose mothers had died from low quality illegal abortions.

While the birth rate initially had exploded as a result of Decree 770, in time, people found ways to resist these state reproductive expectations. For those who could afford it, contraceptives could be found on the black market. Skilled and unskilled abortion providers began to offer their services. The knowledge that this could be incredibly risky was superseded by the reality that another pregnancy could be deadly, and another baby could imperil a family's ability to survive. Hospital septic wards were full of women who had attempted to abort their pregnancies. Maternal and infant death rates skyrocketed, and many women became infertile from botched abortions. Low birth rates and congenital anomalies were common.

People with disabilities did not fit into the nationalist image that the state worked to cultivate, seen as burdensome and unable to contribute as workers to the socialist state. Disabled children were placed in institutions that essentially amount to extermination camps. These facilities lacked heating, electricity, sufficient bed space, medicine, food, and care givers. The children who were sent there were never expected to leave. The mortality rates at these facilities were reportedly around 50%.

Returning to the case of South Korea, during the post-war period abortion laws were not strictly enforced, and instead contraception and sterilization were promoted to reduce fertility rates and control population growth. In addition, permission from male partners was required to access abortion. In 1973, the Mother and Child Act permitted induced abortion under circumstances of rape, incest, and hereditary or genetic "disorders." Consequently, women with disabilities, single mothers, and poor women were targeted and even sometimes coerced into abortion, contraception, or sterilization use. Limiting the fertility of women on the margins, or those who were "undesirable," served as a way to shape the national body according to normative standards of social and economic status. As time went on South Korea's fertility rate slowed and low fertility rates were blamed on anti-natalist polices (Tella, 2023). Abortion as a personal or political issue was rarely discussed in public and carried a social stigma.

Beginning in 2005, population policies shifted as the fertility rate dropped too low—down to 1.08, the lowest in the world at that time (Kim et al., 2019, p. 99). The already existing but unenforced abortion ban in South Korea was revitalized through the passage of the Framework Act on Low Birth Rate in an Aging Society and consequently, anti-abortion groups started to gain momentum. It became common practice for women in need of abortion to travel outside South Korea as practitioners became increasingly worried of prosecution. In 2012 The Constitutional Court upheld the abortion ban citing "the fetus's right to life is in the public interest" and "a woman's right to choose abortion is in an individual interest" therefore "women's rights cannot be more important than the fetus's rights" (Kim et al., 2019, p. 100). This was a blow to women's rights movements in South Korea.

A few years later, in 2015, the Women with Disabilities Empathy formed the Planning Group to Make a New Paradigm for Reproductive Rights for Women with Disabilities. They reviewed various aspects of the criminalization of abortion and concluded that focusing on the single issue of abortion without taking an intersectional approach to advocating for bodily autonomy and freedom for all women, especially women with disabilities, would not be a sufficient or effective strategy to secure reproductive freedom broadly, let alone abortion specifically, and so turned to a reproductive justice framework (Kim, 2023). In 2016, this planning group was reorganized into a coalition of various groups and renamed the Sexual and Reproductive Rights Forum. The Sexual and Reproductive Rights Forum made the argument that "the South Korean government historically had not protected the rights of pregnant women or the lives of fetuses" (Kim, 2023; Kim et al., 2019, p. 100) and had controlled women's bodies and reproductive capacities to advance state interests. They framed issues of abortion as part of a larger context as government control of women's reproductive destinies.

Following protests of an amendment to the Medical Service Act in 2016, which defined abortion as "unethical" and increased penalties for doctors providing abortions, the Sexual and Reproductive Rights Forum held a press conference stating "the real problem is the criminalization of abortion" and "if abortion is a crime, the criminal is the state" (Kim et al., 2019, p. 101). They reinforced the idea that the government has an obligation to ensure sexual and reproductive rights including the right to an abortion and the right to have and raise children regardless of marital status, sexual orientation, ability, or class (Kim, 2023). The Sexual and Reproductive Rights expanded into a new group called the Joint Action for Reproductive Justice in 2017. Their main objective was to challenge and move beyond a pro choice pro life dichotomy. They argued the government has the responsibility to ensure sexual and reproductive health as a human rights issue. The Joint Action for Reproductive Justice came together as a coalition of feminist groups, doctors' organizations, disability rights groups, youth activists, trade unions, political parties, environmental groups, workers' rights groups, and religious groups in South Korea. It included the voices of girls, women living with HIV/AIDS, queer and trans women, and sex workers. Feminist scholars Kim et al. (2019) states, "they aimed to reveal the historical contexts and intersectionality of abortion issues, and in doing so, they intended to clearly establish the decriminalization of abortion as a matter of social justice" (p. 101). Development Studies specialist Tella (2023) echoes this by saying that with the formation of the Joint Action for Reproductive Justice, "The conversation thus moved away from the binary of the foetus versus the mother, but rather acknowledged reproductive rights as a whole and what dignity of life actually included for women, which was autonomy and adequate support, without interference for state interest and control over their sexualities and reproductive bodies" (Tella, 2023, p. 47). The Joint Action for Reproductive Justice maintained a legal strategy of abolishing the criminal codes on abortion. They organized petitions, signature campaigns, and rallies, supported cases that centered on the criminal code on abortion, wrote research papers highlighting women's experiences of abortion, engaged in lobbying efforts, submitted amicus briefs, and held press conferences. Their action garnered support in the form of amicus briefs from the Ministry of Gender Equality and Family, National Human Rights Commission of Korea, Green Party Korea, and Human Rights Watch, The UN Working Group of All Forms of Discrimination Against Women in Law and in Practice and Global Doctors for Choice. Their demands were "(1) fully legalize abortion for the safe termination of pregnancy, (2) expand comprehensive sex education and access to contraceptives, (3) completely revise the eugenic elements of the Mother and Child Health Act, and (4) guarantee reproductive rights without stigma or discrimination" (Kim et al., 2019, p. 103).

On April 11, 2019 the South Korea Constitutional Court ruled that a ban on abortion is unconstitutional. It mandated that the National Assembly revise abortion law by the following year or current criminal codes on abortion would lose effect. The Constitutional Court confirmed that the right to have a child or not have a child was key to a woman's dignity and right to live autonomously. "The justices emphasized that human beings should not be treated as a means for other values, purposes, or legal interests" (Kim et al., 2019, p. 104). The justices also highlighted that social and economic conditions contextualize and influence a woman's reproductive decision-making and therefore the government has a responsibility to support sexual and reproductive human rights through strengthening sex education, counseling, and social welfare for pregnant women and children.

The case of South Korea's struggle over abortion rights and the eventual decriminalization of abortion in 2019 offers a compelling example of how a reproductive justice framework can challenge restrictive legal regimes and reshape national discourse around reproductive autonomy. Unlike traditional pro-choice advocacy, which often centers on the binary of a woman's right to choose versus a fetus's right to life, the reproductive justice approach taken by activists in South Korea redefined the issue in broader, intersectional terms. The Joint Action for Reproductive Justice framed reproductive freedom as deeply connected to structural inequalities shaped by gender, ability, class, sexuality, and national policy. This was a critical shift away from individualized narratives of choice toward a more collective and justice-oriented understanding of reproductive rights as human rights (Kim, 2023).

The feminist coalition's efforts contextualized abortion not as an isolated medical procedure, but as one aspect of a continuum of reproductive experiences that also includes the right to parent, to access adequate healthcare, and to live free from coercive state intervention. The movement emphasized that meaningful reproductive freedom must include access to contraception, comprehensive sex education, support for childbearing and parenting, and the dismantling of eugenic policies embedded in national law. By centering the lived experiences of marginalized populations—such as women with disabilities, single mothers, sex workers, LGBTQ+ individuals, and women living with HIV—the coalition challenged dominant state narratives that had historically devalued certain lives in the pursuit of economic or demographic goals.

Moreover, the South Korean case demonstrates how reproductive justice activism can successfully link grassroots organizing with legal and institutional strategies. The Joint Action for Reproductive Justice not only mobilized mass protests and public education campaigns but also engaged in legal advocacy, research, and lobbying that brought international human rights frameworks to bear on domestic law. Their work drew attention to how the South Korean government had long instrumentalized women's reproductive capacities for state interest, rather than protecting reproductive autonomy as a right in itself.

In essence, the decriminalization of abortion in South Korea was not just a legal victory—it marked a paradigm shift. It acknowledged that reproductive decisions are embedded in social, economic, and political contexts, and that true autonomy can only be realized when the state upholds the conditions necessary for people to make informed and supported choices. This case thus stands as a powerful illustration of reproductive justice in action, offering critical lessons for global feminist movements seeking to move beyond narrow frameworks of rights toward broader visions of justice and dignity.

Conclusion

True control over one's reproductive destiny, including if, when, and how one gives birth, is essential for the well-being of the individual, family, and the community. Bodily integrity is essential to reproductive freedom. In the context of a human rights framework, bodily integrity means that bodily self-determination is a necessary basis for one's full participation in society. Furthermore, bodily integrity translates into the right to "enjoy the full potential of one's body" (Corréa & Petchesky, 1994, p. 107). It is a concept that sees the body as part of an integrated whole self. This sense of self is crucial not only for the individual but for communities and society as a whole. The case studies highlighted in this chapter illustrate the success and social transformation that results from centering bodily integrity vis-à-vis a reproductive justice framework.

This chapter has argued for the urgent necessity of reframing abortion politics within a human rights-based reproductive justice framework—one that moves beyond narrow, neoliberal notions of individual choice to center dignity, equity, and structural change. Grounded in the lived experiences of those most affected by reproductive injustice, this approach illuminates the intersecting oppressions that shape reproductive lives and insists on a collective vision of justice that links bodily autonomy to broader social conditions. As the case studies in the United States, Ireland, and South Korea demonstrate, transformative change emerges when reproductive struggles are situated within a holistic understanding of human rights, intersectionality, and collective care.

The Janes in pre-Roe America, the grassroots coalition behind Ireland's Repeal the 8th campaign, and the Joint Action for Reproductive Justice in South Korea each provide compelling models of what is possible when people resist marginalization and assert their right to reproductive self-determination. These movements succeeded not by relying solely on legal strategies or appeals to individual rights, but by organizing across difference, centering the most impacted, and insisting that reproductive justice is inseparable from racial, economic, and gender justice. Each example reveals the limitations of the "choice" paradigm and the necessity of addressing enabling conditions—such as access to housing, health-care, education, and freedom from violence—as foundational to repro-ductive freedom.

A human rights-based reproductive justice framework offers a powerful tool for resisting state and institutional control over bodies and futures. It affirms that reproductive decisions are never made in a vacuum, but rather within complex matrices of power, oppression, and resistance. To move toward a truly just society, we must insist on structural accountability, cross-movement solidarity, and a commitment to the principle that all people—not just some—deserve the right and resources to make deci-sions about their bodies, families, and futures in safety and dignity.

5

conclusion

The issue of abortion has long served as a mirror reflecting societies' deepest anxieties, inequities, and ideologies. Although a safe and common procedure, across time and culture, abortion has been regulated and restricted because it has the potential to challenge entrenched systems of control over bodies, reproduction, and individual and collective destinies. In this book, we have traced how abortion has been shaped by colonial histories, religious doctrine, medical authority, social class, race, and gender norms. In doing so, it underscores that abortion is not simply about individual decisions but about structural power. It is about who gets to make decisions, under what conditions, and whose lives are legible and deemed worthy of dignity and respect.

As we have shown throughout the preceding chapters, abortion is a common, safe, and necessary form of healthcare. It is also a human rights issue that implicates the right to life, health, privacy, equality, and freedom from cruel, inhuman, and degrading treatment. Globally, however, abortion access remains unequal and deeply politicized. Some people can access high-quality, compassionate care, while others are criminalized, stigmatized, or forced to carry pregnancies against their will. They are the result of policies, cultural narratives, and historical legacies that have prioritized fetal personhood over pregnant people's lives, erased LGBTQ+ and disabled people's experiences, excluded marginalized communities from reproductive decision-making, and are designed to prop up gender and racial hierarchies.

In response, this book advocates for the contextualizing of abortion within a reproductive justice framework—a holistic, intersectional, and human rights-based approach initially developed by Black women in the United States that emphasizes the right not only to abortion, but also to parent, to not parent, and to raise children in safe, supportive environments. Reproductive justice calls for an expansion of the conversation beyond "choice," recognizing that for many people, the ability to make choices is constrained by structural conditions such as poverty, racism, violence, immigration status, and lack of access to healthcare. It reframes abortion not as a moral failure or isolated act but as a component of comprehensive reproductive autonomy.

This framework is essential not only for understanding abortion, but for informing effective, inclusive, and rights-affirming policy. Policymakers and advocates must recognize that abortion access is deeply intertwined with broader issues of social justice. Efforts to restrict abortion often come from the same ideological roots as efforts to suppress sexual and gender minorities, deny healthcare to the poor, and criminalize poverty and pregnancy. Conversely, ensuring access to abortion is part of a broader commitment to justice, equity, and the public good.

From ancient herbal remedies to modern medication abortion, the history of abortion reveals a consistent truth: people have always sought ways to end pregnancies, and they will continue to do so for a wide array of nuanced and complex reasons. The difference lies in whether they are able to access safe, supportive, and legal care. Criminalizing abortion does not stop people from having abortions. It only makes those health care decisions riskier, physiologically or legally.

The case studies presented in this book illustrate the range of ways that communities have organized to challenge unjust laws and expand access to abortion care. In the United States, the Jane Collective exemplified how grassroots, community-led health care can operate even under conditions of criminalization. In Ireland, the Repeal the 8th campaign demonstrates how coalition-building, storytelling, and rights-based discourse can cata-lyze legal change. In South Korea, activists used an intersectional, reproductive justice framework to connect abortion to broader issues of disability rights, LGBTQ+ inclusion, and gender equity.

These movements succeeded not by framing abortion as a narrow single issue, but by making visible the broader conditions that shape reproductive lives such as housing, healthcare, racism, immigration status, and patriarchal violence. They also centered the voices and experiences of those most affected by injustice.

For policymakers, advocates, and activists the implications are clear: abortion advocacy must be grounded in evidence, public health principles, and human rights. Criminalizing abortion does not prevent it; it only makes it less safe. Conversely, when abortion is legal, accessible, and integrated into comprehensive reproductive health care, outcomes improve—not just for individuals, but for families and communities. Institutions such as governments and healthcare systems must also take responsibility for shaping public discourse. Too often, abortion is discussed in polarizing, stigmatizing ways that obscure the realities of people's lives. Public messaging should affirm that abortion is a normal, necessary part of healthcare and that those who seek it deserve respect, privacy, and support.

Legal reform is a necessary starting point but not sufficient on its own. As the Irish and South Korean examples show, even after legal victories, access remains unequal if healthcare systems are underfunded, providers are poorly trained, stigma persists, or marginalized communities remain excluded. Comprehensive reform must include: decriminalization and protection of abortion throughout pregnancy with allowances for individual circumstances and needs; public investment in reproductive health care, including provider training, clinic infrastructure, and services, financial support for abortion services, particularly for low-income individuals; inclusion of diverse communities such as LGBTQ+ individuals, people with disabilities, immigrants etc. in sexual and reproductive health services through gender-affirming, trauma-informed care models; comprehensive sexuality education that includes information about abortion, contraception, consent, and bodily autonomy; supportive services such as childcare, transportation, language translation, and accommodations for disabled people; and international cooperation and accountability to ensure that abortion access is protected in foreign aid and global health policy, including the permanent repeal of harmful policies like the Global Gag Rule.

As this book has argued, we cannot achieve reproductive justice without centering the voices of those most affected by reproductive oppression: Black, Indigenous, and other people of color; disabled people; LGBTQ+ individuals; migrants; incarcerated people; and those living in poverty. Their experiences reveal the compounded barriers to care and the violence of systems that criminalize both reproduction and survival. Governments and institutions must listen to these voices and share power with them in decision-making processes.

The path forward must be intersectional and justice-oriented. Abortion rights cannot be siloed from movements for racial justice, disability justice, LGBTQ+ liberation, workers' rights, and environmental justice. Policymakers and advocates must collaborate across these movements, recognizing that reproductive freedom depends on collective freedom. In addition there must be a move away from stigmatizing, binary, or gender-exclusive language in order to broaden public understanding and build solidarity. Abortion should be regarded as routine healthcare services, not isolated as a specialty or subject to additional scrutiny.

This book asks us to imagine and work toward a world in which reproductive decisions are truly free, supported, and respected. A world where abortion is accessible not just in theory but in practice. A world where no one is forced to carry a pregnancy or parent against their will and people are able to bear and raise the children they have. A world where reproductive freedom is not limited by race, income, nationality, gender, ability, or geography requires a shift towards a reproductive justice framework that centers care, equity, and human dignity. The path to reproductive freedom will not be paved by individual "choices" alone, but by collective struggle, solidarity, and a commitment to justice for all.

references

Abusneineh, B. (2021). (Re)producing the Israeli (European) body: Zionism, anti-Black racism and the Depo-Provera affair. *Feminist Review, 128*(1), 96–113.

Adamczyk, A. (2008). The effects of religious contextual norms, structural constraints, and personal religiosity on abortion decisions. *Social Science Research, 37*(2), 657–672.

American College of Obstetricians and Gynecologists. (2015). *ACOG statement regarding abortion procedure bans.* https://www.acog.org/news/news-releases/2015/10/acog-statement-regarding-abortion-procedure-bans

American College of Obstetricians and Gynecologists. (2020). *Medication abortion up to 70 days of gestation.* https://www.acog.org/clinical/clinical-guidance/practice-bulletin/articles/2020/10/medication-abortion-up-to-70-days-of-gestation

American College of Obstetricians and Gynecologists. (2022a). *Facts are important: Understanding abortion later in pregnancy.* https://www.acog.org/advocacy/facts-are-important/understanding-abortion-later-in-pregnancy

American College of Obstetricians and Gynecologists. (2022b). *Abortion and perinatal palliative care.* https://www.acog.org/advocacy/facts-are-important/abortion-and-perinatal-palliative-care

American College of Obstetricians and Gynecologists. (n.d.). *Facts are important: Abortion and perinatal palliative care.* https://www.acog.org/advocacy/facts-are-important/abortion-and-perinatal-palliative-care

Amnesty International. (2021). *An unstoppable movement: A global call to recognize and protect those who defend the right to abortion.* https://www.amnesty.org/en/documents/act30/4205/2021/en/

Armstrong, E. M. (2003). *Conceiving risk, bearing responsibility: Fetal alcohol syndrome and the diagnosis of moral disorder.* Johns Hopkins University Press.

Baker, C. N. (2024). *Abortion pills: US history and politics.* Amherst College Press.

Bakhru, T. S. (2017). Reproductive health and human rights: Lessons from Ireland. *Journal of International Women's Studies, 18222,* 27–44.

Bankole, A., Singh, S., & Haas, T. (1998). Reasons why women have induced abortions: Evidence from 27 countries. *International Family Planning*

Perspectives, 24(3), 117–127 & 152. https://www.guttmacher.org/journals/ipsrh/1998/09/reasons-why-women-have-induced-abortions-evidence-27-countries

Bart, P. B. (1987). Seizing the means of reproduction: An illegal feminist abortion collective—how and why it worked. *Qualitative Sociology, 10*(4), 339–357.

Bearak, J., Popinchalk, A., Ganatra, B., Moller, A.-B., Tunçalp, Ö., Beavin, C., Kwok, L., & Alkema, L. (2020). Unintended pregnancy and abortion by income, region, and the legal status of abortion: Estimates from a comprehensive model for 1990–2019. *The Lancet Global Health, 8*(9), e1152–e1161.

Berer, M. (2004). Sexuality, rights and social justice. *Reproductive Health Matters, 12*(23), 6–11.

Bi, S., & Klusty, T. (2015). Forced sterilizations of HIV-positive women: A global ethics and policy failure. *AMA Journal of Ethics, 17*(10), 952–957.

Braine, N. (2023). *Abortion beyond the law: Building a global feminist movement for self-managed abortion.* Verso Books.

Briggs, L. (2017). *How all politics became reproductive politics: From welfare reform to foreclosure to Trump.* University of California Press.

Buyse, A. (2018). Squeezing civic space: Restrictions on civil society organizations and the linkages with human rights. *The International Journal of Human Rights, 22*(8), 966–988.

Caldwell, E. C. (2016, July 15). The history of "Your body is a battleground". *JSTOR Daily.* https://daily.jstor.org/the-history-your-body-is-a-battleground/

Calkin, S. (2023). *Abortion pills go global: Reproductive freedom across borders* (Vol. 7). Univ of California Press.

Callender, B., & Carlyle, M. (2019). *The fetus in utero: From mystery to social media. KNOW: A Journal on the Formation of Knowledge, 3*(1), 15–67. https://www.academia.edu/38774580/The_Fetus_in_Utero_From_Mystery_to_Social_Media

Callender, B., Carlyle, M., & Chor, J. (2021). The power and politics of fetal imagery. *Lancet (London, England), 398*(10307), 1208–1209.

Campbell, S. (2013). A short history of sonography in obstetrics and gynaecology. *Facts, Views & Vision in ObGyn, 5*(3), 213.

Casper, M. J. (2022). *Babylost: Racism, survival, and the quiet politics of infant mortality, from A to Z.* Rutgers University Press.

Centers for Disease Control and Prevention. (2022, November 25). *Abortion surveillance — United States, 2020* (Vol. 71, No. 10). U.S. Department of Health and Human Services. https://stacks.cdc.gov/view/cdc/123183

Center for Reproductive Rights. (2024). *Abortion* (or other specific page title if available). https://reproductiverights.org/our-issues/abortion/

Center for Reproductive Rights. (n.d.). *The world's abortion laws.* https://reproductiverights.org/maps/worlds-abortion-laws/. Retrieved June 20, 2025.

Chae, S., Desai, S., Crowell, M., Sedgh, G., & Singh, S. (2017). Reasons why women have induced abortions: A synthesis of findings from 14 countries. *Contraception*, *96*(4), 233–241.

Chasen, S. T., Kalish, R. B., Gupta, M., Kaufman, J. E., Rashbaum, W. K., & Chervenak, F. A. (2004). Dilation and evacuation at ≥20 weeks: Comparison of operative techniques. *American Journal of Obstetrics and Gynecology*, *190*(5), 1180–1183.

Chrisler, J. C. (Ed.). (2012). *Reproductive justice: A global concern*. Praeger/ABC-CLIO.

Cook, R. J., Dickens, B. M., & Fathalla, M. F. (2003). *Reproductive health and human rights: Integrating medicine, ethics, and law*. Oxford University Press.

Cook, R., Erdman, J., & Dickens, B. (2014). *Abortion law in transnational perspectives: Cases and controversies*. University of Pennsylvania Press.

Corrêa, S., & Petchesky, R. (1994). Reproductive and sexual rights: A feminist perspective. In G. Sen, A. Germain, & L. C. Chen (Eds.), *Population policies reconsidered: Health, empowerment, and rights* (pp. 107–123). Harvard University Press.

Corrêa, S., & Reichmann, R. (1994). *Population and reproductive rights: Feminist perspectives from the South*. Zed Books.

Cramer, R. A. (2021). *Birthing a movement: Midwives, law, and the politics of reproductive care*. Stanford University Press.

Crenshaw, K. (2017). *On intersectionality: Essential writings*. The New Press.

Daniels, C. R., Ferguson, J., Howard, G., & Roberti, A. (2016). Informed or misinformed consent? Abortion policy in the United States. *Journal of Health Politics, Policy and Law*, *41*(2), 181–209.

Danielsen, S. (2021). Mobilizing on abortion: Social networks, civil disobedience, and the clergy consultation service on abortion, 1967–1973. *Journal of Church and State*, *63*(3), 461–484.

De Londras, F., & Enright, M. (2018). *Repealing the 8th: Reforming Irish abortion law*. Policy Press.

Dirks, D. A., & Relf, P. A. (2017). *To offer compassion: A history of the clergy consultation service on abortion*. University of Wisconsin Press.

Donald, I., MacVicar, J., & Brown, T. G. (1958). Investigation of abdominal masses by pulsed ultrasound. *The Lancet*, *271*(7032), 1188–1195.

du Prey, B. (2008). Reflections on the history of abortion. In *Proceedings of the 17th annual history of medicine days*.

Dubow, S. (2010). *Ourselves unborn: A history of the fetus in modern America*. Oxford University Press.

Duffy, D. N. (2020). From feminist anarchy to decolonisation: Understanding abortion health activism before and after the repeal of the 8th Amendment. *Feminist Review*, *124*(1), 69–85.

Enright, M., Conway, V., de Londras, F., Donnelly, M., Fletcher, R., McDonnell, N., McGuinness, S., Murray, C., Ring, S., & Uí Chonnachtaigh, S. (2015). *feminists@ law, 5*(1). http://journals.kent.ac.uk/index.php/feministsatlaw/article/view/173/631

Esacove, A. W. (2004). Dialogic framing: The framing/counterframing of "partial-birth" abortion. *Sociological Inquiry, 74*(1), 70-101.

Fallon, B. (2012). Protesters in Ireland rally for abortion rights. *CNN World+*. http://www.cnn.com/2012/11/17/world/europe/ireland-abortion-controversy/

Fetters, T., Rubayet, S., Sultana, S., Nahar, S., Tofigh, S., Jones, L., Samandari, G., & Powell, B. (2020). Navigating the crisis landscape: Engaging the Ministry of Health and United Nations agencies to make abortion care available to Rohingya refugees. *Conflict and Health, 14*, Article 50.

Finer, L. B., Frohwirth, L. F., Dauphinee, L. A., Singh, S., & Moore, A. M. (2005). Reasons US women have abortions: Quantitative and qualitative perspectives. *Perspectives on Sexual and Reproductive Health, 37*(3), 110–118. https://doi.org/10.1363/psrh.37.110.05

Fischer, B. (2016). See Jane decide: The feminist abortion service contemplates an evolution. *Women Leading Change: Case Studies on Women, Gender, and Feminism, 1*(1), 40–49.

Flavin, J. (2008). Our bodies, our crimes: The policing of women's reproduction in America. In *Our bodies, our crimes*. New York University Press.

Flavin, J., & Paltrow, L. M. (2010). Punishing pregnant drug-using women: Defying law, medicine, and common sense. *Journal of Addictive Diseases, 29*(2), 231–244.

Frank, G. (2025). The pastoral was political: Religious rights and reproductive freedom before Roe. *Journal of the American Academy of Religion, 93*(2), Ifaf051.

Frank, G., Ghanoui, S. L., & Gutterman, L. J. (2023). Sex with the sound on. *The American Historical Review, 128*(2), 691–701.

Fuentes, L. (2023). *Inequity in U.S. abortion rights and access: The end of Roe is deepening existing divides*. Guttmacher Institute. https://www.guttmacher.org/commentary/2023/06/inequity-us-abortion-rights-and-access-end-roe-deepening-existing-divides

Ganatra, B. (2008). Maintaining access to safe abortion and reducing sex ratio imbalances in Asia. *Reproductive Health Matters, 16*(31), 90–98.

Goodwin, M. (2020). *Policing the womb: Invisible women and the criminalization of motherhood*. Cambridge University Press.

Gould, S. J. (1985). Carrie Buck's daughter. *Constitutional Commentary, 2*, 331.

Government of Canada. (2023, May 9). *Improving access to abortion services and information under the sexual and reproductive health fund*. https://www.canada.ca/en/health-canada/news/2023/05/improving-access-to-abortion-services-and-information-under-the-sexual-and-reproductive-health-fund.html

Graff, A. (2014). Report from the gender trenches: War against "genderism" in Poland. *European Journal of Women's Studies*, 21(4), 431–435.

Grescoe, T. (2022). This miracle plant was eaten into extinction 2000 years ago. Or was it?. *National Geographic*. https://www.nationalgeographic.com/premium/article/miracle-plant-eaten-extinction-2000-years-ago-silphion

Guilmoto, C. Z. (2012). Son preference, sex selection, and kinship in Vietnam. *Population and Development Review*, 38(1), 31–54.

Gutierrez-Romine, A. (2020). *From Back Alley to the border: Criminal abortion in California, 1920-196*. U of Nebraska Press.

Guttmacher Institute. (2018). *Induced abortion worldwide: Global incidence and trends*. https://www.guttmacher.org/fact-sheet/induced-abortion-worldwide-2018

Guttmacher Institute. (2022a). *Abortion worldwide 2022: Uneven progress and unequal access*. https://www.guttmacher.org/report/abortion-worldwide-2022

Guttmacher Institute. (2022b). *Abortion patients by sexual orientation*. https://www.guttmacher.org/fact-sheet/abortion-patients-sexual-orientation

Guttmacher Institute. (n.d.). *The global Gag Rule and the Helms Amendment: What do these policies do?*.https://www.guttmacher.org/fact-sheet/ggr-helms-amendment

Haddad, L. B., & Nour, N. M. (2009). Unsafe abortion: Unnecessary maternal mortality. *Reviews in Obstetrics & Gynecology*, 2(2), 122–126.

Hampe, A., & Petit, R. J. (2010). Cryptic forest refugia on the 'Roof of the World'. *New Phytologist*, 185(1), 5–7.

Health, Information, and Quality Authority. (2013). *Patient safety investigation report published by health information and quality authority*. http://www.hiqa.ie/press-release/2013-10-09-patient-safety-investigation-report-published-health-information-and-qualit

Hepburn, M. A. (2014). *Lives worthy of life and remembrance: Memorialization of the national socialist Aktion T4 euthanasia programme* (Doctoral dissertation).

Hesketh, T., Lu, L., & Xing, Z. W. (2005). The effect of China's one-child family policy after 25 years. *New England Journal of Medicine*, 353(11), 1171–1176.

Higgins, A. (2020). Dawn Wooten alleges forced hysterectomies at an ICE detention center: The US has a brutal history of forced sterilizations. *The Washington Post*. https://www.washingtonpost.com/gender-identity/a-whistleblower-alleges-mass-hysterectomies-at-an-ice-detention-center-the-us-has-a-brutal-history-of-forced-sterilizations/

Holland, K. (2014). College tells psychiatrists not to do abortion assessments: Psychiatrists say implementation of new abortion Act 'completely unsatisfactory'. *The Irish Times*. http://www.irishtimes.com/news/social-affairs/college-tells-psychiatrists-not-to-do-abortion-assessments-1.1642834

Howard, G. E. (2023). Weaponizing the law to punish people for miscarriage. *Ms. Magazine*. https://msmagazine.com/2023/12/12/miscarriage-crime-nonviable-fetus-crime-ohio-texas/

Howard, G. E. (2024). *The pregnancy police: Conceiving crime, arresting personhood* (Vol. 10). Univ of California Press.

HSE Sexual Health & Crisis Pregnancy Programme. (2015). *Number of women giving Irish addresses at UK abortion clinics decreases for tenth year in a row according to Department of Health UK*. HSE Crisis Pregnancy Programme. http://www.crisispregnancy.ie/news/number-of-women-giving-irish-addresses-at-uk-abortion-clinics-decreases-for-tenth-year-in-a-row-according-to-department-of-health-uk/

Human Rights Watch. (2011). *Sterilization of women and girls with disabilities, a briefing paper*. https://www.hrw.org/news/2011/11/10/sterilization-women-and-girls-disabilities

Hurst, D. (2019). Victims of forced sterilization in Japan to receive compensation and apology. *The Guardian*. https://www.theguardian.com/world/2019/mar/18/victims-of-forced-sterilisation-in-japan-to-receive-compensation-and-apology

Hurst, R. (2020). *Representing abortion*. Routledge.

Irish Family Planning Association. (2004). *Abortion in Ireland: Legal timeline*. https://www.ifpa.ie/advocacy/abortion-in-ireland-legal-timeline/

Irish Family Planning Association. (n.d.). *Abortion in Ireland: Legal timeline*. Retrieved July 24, 2025, from.https://www.ifpa.ie/advocacy/abortion-in-ireland-legal-timeline/

Jones, R. K., Chiu, D. W., & Kohn, J. E. (2023). Characteristics of people obtaining medication vs procedural abortions in clinical settings in the United States: Findings from the 2021–2022 abortion patient survey. *Contraception, 118*, 110137. https://doi.org/10.1016/j.contraception.2023.110137

Jones, R. K., & Karnik, A. F. (2024). *Medication abortion accounted for 63% of all us abortions in 2023—an increase from 53% in 2020*. https://www.guttmacher.org/2024/03/medication-abortion-accounted-63-all-us-abortions-2023-increase-53-2020

Jones, R. K., Kirstein, M., & Philbin, J. (2022). Abortion incidence and service availability in the United States, 2020. *Perspectives on Sexual and Reproductive Health, 54*(4), 128–141.

Joyce, T. J., Henshaw, S. K., Dennis, A., Finer, L. B., & Blanchard, K. (2009). *The impact of state mandatory counseling and waiting period laws on abortion: A literature review*. Guttmacher. https://www.guttmacher.org/sites/default/files/pdfs/pubs/MandatoryCounseling.pdf

Kaplan, L. (2019). *The story of Jane: The legendary underground feminist abortion service*. University of Chicago Press.

Kapp, N., Andersen, K., Griffin, R., Handayani, A. P., Schellekens, M., & Gomperts, R. (2021). Medical abortion at 13 or more weeks gestation provided through telemedicine: A retrospective review of services. *Contraception X, 3*, 100057.

Kennedy, S. (2018). "#Repealthe8th": Ireland, abortion access and the movement to remove the Eighth Amendment. *Antropologia, 5*(2), 13–31.

Kim, S. (2023, February 7). *From population control to reproductive justice.* Verfassungsblog. https://verfassungsblog.de/from-population-control-to-reproductive-justice/

Kim, S., Young, N., & Lee, Y. (2019). The role of reproductive justice movements in challenging South Korea's abortion ban. *Health and Human Rights, 21*(2), 97–107.

King, C. R. (1993). Calling Jane: The life and death of a women's illegal abortion service. *Women & Health, 20*(3), 75–93.

Klautke, E. (2016). 'The Germans are beating us at our own game' American eugenics and the German sterilization law of 1933. *History of the Human Sciences, 29*(3), 25–43.

Kolbert, K., & Kay, J. F. (2021). *Controlling women: What we must do now to save reproductive freedom.* Hachette Books.

Kruger, B. (1989). (Untitled) Your body is a battleground [Silkscreen on vinyl]. *The Broad.* https://www.thebroad.org/art/barbara-kruger/untitled-your-body-battleground

Lawrence, J. (2000). The Indian health service and the sterilization of Native American women. *American Indian Quarterly, 24*(3), 400–419.

Lentin, R. (2013). A woman died: Abortion and the politics of birth in Ireland. *Feminist Review, 105*(1), 130–136.

Lewis, C. S. (2025). *American infanticide: Sexism, science, and the politics of sympathy.* Rutgers University Press.

Lombardo, P. A. (2008). Disability, eugenics, and the culture wars. *Louis University Journal of Health Law & Policy, 2*, 57.

Lopatka, J., (2024). Czech court removes surgery requirement for gender. *Reuters.* https://www.reuters.com/world/europe/czech-court-removes-surgery-requirement-gender-transition-2024-05-07/

Lowik, A. J. (2022). *Trans-inclusive abortion services: A manual for providers.* Fédération du Québec pour le planning des naissances (FQPN).

Luna, Z. T. (2020). *Reproductive rights as human rights: Women of color and the fight for reproductive justice.* New York University Press.

Maddow-Zimet, I., & Gibson, C. (2024). *Despite bans, number of abortions in the United States increased in 2023.* Guttmacher. https://www.guttmacher.org/2024/03/despite-bans-number-abortions-united-states-increased-2023

Mohapatra, S. (2011). Unshackling addiction: A public health approach to drug use during pregnancy. *Wisconsin Journal of Gender, & Society, 26*, 241.

Morone, J. A. (1997). Enemies of the people: The moral dimension to public health. *Journal of Health Politics, Policy and Law*, *22*(4), 993–1020.

Morrow, M. (2022) Abortion throughout history: From ancient Greece to post-Roe America. *The Indypendent*. Issue 273. https://indypendent.org/2022/08/abortion-throughout-history/

Moseson, H., Fix, L., Gerdts, C., Stoeffler, A., Hastings, J., & Hunter, L. (2021). Abortion experiences and preferences of transgender, nonbinary, and gender-expansive people in the United States. *American Journal of Obstetrics & Gynecology*, *224*(4), 376.e1–376.e11.

Moseson, H., Jayaweera, R., Egwuatu, I., Grosso, B., Kristianingrum, I. A., Nmezi, S., Zurbriggen, R., Motana, R., Bercu, C., Carbone, S., & Gerdts, C. (2022). Effectiveness of self-managed medication abortion with accompaniment support in Argentina and Nigeria (SAFE): a prospective, observational cohort study and non-inferiority analysis with historical controls. *The Lancet Global Health*, *10*(1), e105–e113.

Murphy, S., & Rosenbaum, M. (1999). *Pregnant women on drugs: Combating stereotypes and stigma*. Rutgers University Press.

Murray, A. F. (2008). *From outrage to courage: Women taking action for health and justice* (x, p. 311). Common Courage Press.

Nanda, B. (2018). A syncretic feminist approach. In *Discourse on rights in India: Debates and dilemmas*. Routledge.

National Abortion Federation. (2024). *Clinical policy guidelines for abortion care*. https://prochoice.org/wp-content/uploads/2024-CPGs-FINAL-1.pdf

National Abortion Federation. (2025). *2024 Violence and disruption report*. https://prochoice.org/our-work/provider-security/2024-naf-violence-disruption/

National Academies of Sciences, Engineering, and Medicine. (2018). *The safety and quality of abortion care in the United States*. The National Academies Press. https://nap.nationalacademies.org/catalog/24950/the-safety-and-quality-of-abortion-care-in-the-united-states

Obstetric and Gynecological Consultative Committee. (2018). *Misoprostol only recommended regime*. World Health Organization. https://platform.who.int/docs/default-source/mca-documents/policy-documents/operational-guidance/IRQ-MN-32-03-OPERATIONALGUIDANCE-2018-eng-Misoprostol-Recommended-Regime.pdf

Ocen, P. A. (2017). Birthing injustice: Pregnancy as a status offense. *The George Washington Law Review*, *85*, 1163.

OHCHR, UNFPA, UNICEF, UN Women, & WHO. (2012). *Unsafe abortion: The preventable pandemic [Joint interagency statement]*. World Health Organization. https://www.who.int/publications/i/item/unsafe-abortion-the-preventable-pandemic

Open Society Foundation. (2011). *Against her will: Forced and coerced sterilization of women worldwide*. https://www.opensocietyfoundations.org/publications/against-her-will-forced-and-coerced-sterilization-women-worldwide

Open Society Foundation. (2015). *License to be yourself: Forced sterilization*. https://www.opensocietyfoundations.org/publications/forced-sterilization

OpenDemocracy. (2020). *Trump-linked religious extremists spreading disinformation on pregnant women worldwide*. https://www.opendemocracy.net/en/5050/trump-linked-religious-extremists-global-disinformation-pregnant-women/

Otsubo, S., & Bartholomew, J. R. (1998). Eugenics in Japan: Some ironies of modernity, 1883–1945. *Science in Context, 11*(3–4), 545–565.

Owens, D. C. (2017). *Medical bondage: Race, gender, and the origins of American gynecology*. University of Georgia Press.

Paltrow, L. M., & Flavin, J. (2013). Arrests of and forced interventions on pregnant women in the United States, 1973–2005: Implications for women's legal status and public health. *Journal of Health Politics, Policy and Law, 38*(2), 299–343.

Partridge, J. C. (2022). Definitions of viability and their meaning for neonatal care. In *Abortion care as moral work* (pp. 170–176). Rutgers University Press.

Petchesky, R. P. (2003). *Global prescriptions: Gendering health and human rights*. Zed Books.

Pfafflin, F. (1986). The connections between eugenics, sterilization and mass murder in Germany from 1933 to 1945. *Medicine and Law, 5*, 1.

Puri, M., Rocca, C., Blum, M., Harper, C., Joshi, D., & Henderson, J. (2011). Post-abortion contraceptive use and continuation in Nepal. *Contraception, 83*(1), 82–86.

Rahm, L. (2020). Gender-biased sex selection in South Korea, India and Vietnam: Assessing the influence of public policy. In *Demographic transformation and socio-economic development* (Vol. 11). Springer.

Raymond, E. G., Mark, A., Grossman, D., Beasley, A., Brandi, K., Castle, J., Crenin, M. D., Gerdts, C., Gil, L., Grant, M., Lockley, A., Perrit, J., Shochet, T., Truan, D., & Upadhyay, U. D. (2023). Medication abortion with misoprostol-only: A sample protocol. *Contraception, 121*, 109998.

Reagan, L. J. (1997). *When abortion was a crime: Women, medicine, and law in the United States, 1867–1973*. University of California Press.

Rebouché, R. (2017). Reproducing rights: The intersection of reproductive justice and human rights. *UC Irvine Law Review, 7*, 579.

Redden, M. (2016). Purvi Patel has 20-year sentence for inducing own abortion reduced. *The Guardian*. https://www.theguardian.com/us-news/2016/jul/22/purvi-patel-abortion-sentence-reduced

Riddle, J. M. (1999). *Eve's herbs: A history of contraception and abortion in the west*. Harvard University Press.

Roberts, D. E. (1990). Punishing drug addicts who have babies: Women of color, equality, and the right of privacy. *Harvard Law Review, 104,* 1419.

Roberts, D. E. 1992. Crime, race, and reproduction. *Tulsa Law Review, 67,* 1945.

Roberts, D. E. (1996). Unshackling black motherhood. *Michigan Law Review, 95,* 938.

Roberts, D. E. (2014). *Killing the black body: Race, reproduction, and the meaning of liberty.* Vintage.

Ross, L. (2020). Understanding reproductive justice. In *Feminist theory reader* (pp. 77–82). Routledge.

Ross, L., Gutiérrez, E., Gerber, M., & Silliman, J. (2016). *Undivided rights: Women of color organizing for reproductive justice.* Haymarket Books.

Ross, L., Roberts, L., Derkas, E., Peoples, W., & Bridgewater Toure, P. (Eds.). (2017). *Radical reproductive justice: Foundations, theory, practice, critique.* Feminist Press at the City University of New York.

Ross, L., & Solinger, R. (2017). *Reproductive justice: An introduction* (Vol. 1). Univ of California Press.

Rowlands, S., Heaslip, V., Felske-Durksen, C., Carranza Ko, Ñ., Albert, G., Rich, R., Black, K. A., & Szilvási, M. (2025). The forced sterilisation of indigenous and racialised peoples: Origins, nature of abuses, impacts and responses. *International Perspectives on Health Equity, 1*(1), 1–20.

Schoen, J. (2019). Abortion care as moral work. *Journal of Modern European History, 17*(3), 262–279.

Scott, M. S. (1996). Quickening in the common law: The legal precedent Roe attempted and failed to use. *Michigan Law & Policy Review, 1,* 199–223.

Seager, J. (2018). *The women's atlas* (5th ed.). Penguin Books.

Sedgh, G., Singh, S., Shah, I. H., Åhman, E., Henshaw, S. K., & Bankole, A. (2012). Induced abortion: Incidence and trends worldwide from 1995 to 2008. *The Lancet, 379*(9816), 625–632. https://www.thelancet.com/journals/lancet/article/PIIS0140-6736(11)61786-8/abstract

Sella, S. (2025). *Beyond limits: Stories of third-trimester abortion care.* Penguin Random House.

Sherbourne Health. (2023, May 9). *Sherbourne receives federal funding to improve reproductive health access for 2SLGBTQI+ people.* Rainbow Health Ontario. https://www.rainbowhealthontario.ca/sherbourne-receives-federal-funding-to-improve-reproductive-health-access-for-2slgbtqi-people/

Sherman, C., (2025). Baby of brain-dead Georgia woman on life support delivered via c-section. *The Guardian.* https://www.theguardian.com/us-news/2025/jun/17/brain-dead-georgia-woman-delivers-baby

Sherman, R. B., & Mahone, R. (2024). *Liberating abortion: Claiming our history, sharing our stories, and building the reproductive future we deserve.* Amistad.

Silverstein, H. (2001). In the matter of anonymous, a minor: Fetal representation in hearings to waive parental consent for abortion. *Cornell Journal of Law and Public Policy, 11*, 69.

Singh, S., Remez, L., Sedgh, G., Kwok, L., & Onda, T. (2018). *Abortion worldwide 2017: Uneven progress and unequal access*. Guttmacher Institute. https://www.guttmacher.org/report/abortion-worldwide-2017

Skuster, P., Sully, E. A., & Friedrich-Karnik, A. (2020). *Evidence for ending the global gag rule: A multiyear study in two countries*. Guttmacher Institute. https://www.guttmacher.org/report/evidence-for-ending-global-gag-rule

Smith, A. (2005). Beyond pro-choice versus pro-life: Women of color and reproductive justice. *NWSA Journal, 17*(1), 119–140.

Society of Family Planning. (2025). *#WeCount report April 2022 through December 2024*. https://societyfp.org/wecount-report-9-december-2024-data/

Solinger, R. (2001). But no faith in the people. *Social Justice, 28*(1[83]), 11–13.

Solinger, R. (2013). *Reproductive politics*. Oxford University Press.

Solinger, R. (2019). *The abortionist: A woman against the law*. University of California Press.

Sommer, U., & Forman-Rabinovici, A. (2019). *Producing reproductive rights: Determining abortion policy worldwide*. Cambridge University Press; Hurst, R. (2020). Representing Abortion. Routledge.

Stern, A. M. (2005). Sterilized in the name of public health: Race, immigration, and reproductive control in modern California. *American Journal of Public Health, 95*(7), 1128–1138.

Stern, A. M. (2022). From "race suicide" to "white extinction": White nationalism, nativism, and eugenics over the past century. *Journal of American History, 109*(2), 348–361.

Strange, C., & Stephen, J. A., (2012). Eugenics in Canada: A checkered history, 1850s-1990s, in *The Oxford handbook of the history of eugenics*. Oxford Academic.

Tella, K. K. (2023). *Abortion rights, reproductive justice and the state: International perspectives* (1st ed.). Routledge India.

Theobald, B. (2019). *Reproduction on the reservation: Pregnancy, childbirth, and colonialism in the long twentieth century*. UNC Press.

Tydén, M., (2012). The Scandinavian states: Reformed eugenics applied. In *Oxford handbook of the history of eugenics*. Oxford Academic.

United Nations. (1948). *Universal declaration of human rights*. https://www.un.org/en/about-us/universal-declaration-of-human-rights

United Nations Population Fund. (1994). *Programme of action of the international conference on population and development*. United Nations Population Fund.

United Nations Population Fund. (2001). *Reproductive health for communities in crisis: UNFPA emergency response*. UNFPA.

United Nations Population Fund. (2020). *State of world population 2020: Defying the practices that harm women and girls and undermine equality*. https://www.unfpa.org/sites/default/files/pub-pdf/UNFPA_PUB_2020_EN_State_of_World_Population.pdf

United Nations Population Fund. (2023). *Crisis response and women's health*. https://www.unfpa.org/resources/crisis-response-and-womens-health

Visaria, L. (2000). Reproductive health in policy and practice: India's population policy and family planning programme. In *The IUSSP conference on family planning in the 21st century*.

Waterfield, B. (2013, June 13) *Irish abortion law key factor in death of Savita Halappanavar, official report finds*. The Telegraph. http://www.telegraph.co.uk/news/worldnews/europe/ireland/10119109/Irish-abortion-law-key-factor-in-death-of-Savita-Halappanavar-official-report-finds.html

Whelan, A. (n.d.). *An inclusive approach to LGBTQ+ abortion rights*. Advocates for Youth. https://www.advocatesforyouth.org/resources/health-justice/an-inclusive-approach-to-lgbtq-abortion-rights/

Whiteley, R. (2023). *Birth figures: Early modern prints and the pregnant body*. University of Chicago Press.

Wingo, E., Ingraham, N., & Roberts, S. C. M. (2018). Reproductive health care priorities and barriers to effective care for LGBTQ people assigned female at birth: A qualitative study in four U.S. and Canadian cities. *Health Services Research, 53*(6), 4198–4215.

World Health Organization. (2019). *Medical management of abortion*. https://www.who.int/publications/i/item/9789241550406

World Health Organization. (2021, September 28). *Abortion*. https://www.who.int/news-room/fact-sheets/detail/abortion

World Health Organization. (2022). *Abortion care guideline*. https://www.who.int/publications/i/item/9789240039483

World Health Organization. (2024a). *Sexual and reproductive health for all: 20 years of the global strategy*. https://www.who.int/news/item/16-05-2024-sexual-and-reproductive-health-for-all-20-years-of-the-global-strategy

World Health Organization. (2024b). *Abortion*. https://www.who.int/news-room/fact-sheets/detail/abortion

World Health Organization. (n.d.-a). *Human rights and health*. https://www.who.int/news-room/fact-sheets/detail/human-rights-and-health

World Health Organization. (n.d.-b). *Sexual and reproductive health and rights*. https://www.who.int/health-topics/sexual-and-reproductive-health-and-rights

index